Find us onlir

C000184758

GOV.UK – Simpler, clear

GOV.UK is the best place to find government services and information for

- car drivers
- motorcyclists
- driving licences
- driving and riding tests
- towing a caravan or trailer
- medical rules
- driving and riding for a living
- online services.

Visit **www.gov.uk** and try it out.

You can also find contact details for DVSA and other motoring agencies like DVLA at **www.gov.uk**

You'll notice that links to **GOV.UK**, the UK's central government site, do not always take you to a specific page. This is because this kind of site constantly adapts to what people really search for. So such static links would quickly go out of date. Try it out. Simply search what you need from your preferred search site or from **www.gov.uk** and you should find what you're looking for. You can give feedback to the Government Digital Service from the website.

Driver & Vehicle
Standards
Agency

The **Official DVSA Guide** to
Learning
to Drive

London: TSO

Written and compiled by the Learning Materials section of the Driver and Vehicle Standards Agency (DVSA).

© Crown Copyright 2019

All rights reserved. No part of this publication may be reproduced in any material form without the written permission of the copyright owner except in accordance with the provisions of the Copyright, Designs and Patents Act 1988 or under the terms of a licence issued by the Copyright Licensing Agency Ltd. Crown Copyright material is reproduced with permission of the Keeper of the Public Record.

Previously known as *Your Driving Test* (First edition 1990) and *The Official Driving Test* (Third edition 1996)

Current title: *The Official DVSA Guide to Learning to Drive*

Eleventh edition 2019
Fifth impression 2021

ISBN 978 0 11 5536595

A CIP catalogue record for this book is available from the British Library.

Other titles in the Driving Skills series

The Official DVSA Guide to Driving – the essential skills
The Official DVSA Guide to Better Driving
The Official DVSA Theory Test for Car Drivers
The Official DVSA Theory Test for Car Drivers (DVD-ROM)
The Official DVSA Guide to Hazard Perception (DVD-ROM)

The Official DVSA Theory Test Kit iPhone/Android App
The Official DVSA Highway Code iPhone App
The Official DVSA Hazard Perception Practice iOS/Android App

The Official DVSA Guide to Riding – the essential skills
The Official DVSA Theory Test for Motorcyclists
The Official DVSA Theory Test for Motorcyclists (DVD-ROM)
The Official DVSA Guide to Learning to Ride
Better Biking – the official DVSA training aid (DVD)

The Official DVSA Guide to Driving Buses and Coaches
The Official DVSA Guide to Driving Goods Vehicles
The Official DVSA Theory Test for Drivers of Large Vehicles
The Official DVSA Theory Test for Drivers of Large Vehicles (DVD-ROM)
Driver CPC – the official DVSA guide for professional bus and coach drivers
Driver CPC – the official DVSA guide for professional goods vehicle drivers

The Official DVSA Guide to Tractor and Specialist Vehicle Driving Tests (eBook)

The Official DVSA Theory Test for Approved Driving Instructors (DVD-ROM)

Every effort has been made to ensure that the information contained in this publication is accurate at the time of going to press. The Stationery Office cannot be held responsible for any inaccuracies. Information in this book is for guidance only.

All metric and imperial conversions in this book are approximate.

Rules on driving and operating in the European Union (EU) may change during the Brexit transition. Check **www.gov.uk/transition** for the latest information.

We're turning over a new leaf.

RECYCLED
Paper made from recycled material
FSC® C002151

Message from Mark Winn, the Chief Driving Examiner

Being able to drive on your own opens up a whole new world of independence. But, before you apply to take your practical test, you must have the skills and mindset you'll need to drive independently.

In this book, we explain the skills you need to understand and master before taking your test. We refer to the 'Driver's Record'; if you do not have one of these, ask your instructor for a copy, or you can download one from **www.gov.uk**

You need to be capable of driving consistently, without help or prompting, and achieve all the key skills in the 'Driver's Record' before you take your practical test. Most people fail their test because they're not fully prepared, so make sure that you've covered all the key skills to the standard we show in this book.

The best way to gain these skills is to take enough lessons with an approved driving instructor and get plenty of practice. You should aim to gain experience driving in varying traffic conditions, on different types of road and under a wide range of differing weather conditions.

Once you have the relevant skills and experience, and you've developed the right attitude, you'll be ready for a lifetime of safe driving.

Mark Winn
Chief Driving Examiner

Driver & Vehicle Standards Agency

The Driver and Vehicle Standards Agency (DVSA) is an executive agency of the Department for Transport.

We improve road safety in Great Britain by setting standards for driving and motorcycling, and making sure drivers, vehicle operators and MOT garages understand and follow roadworthiness standards. We also provide a range of licensing, testing, education and enforcement services.

www.gov.uk/dvsa

The Driver and Vehicle Agency (DVA) is an executive agency within the Department of the Environment for Northern Ireland.

Its primary aim is to promote and improve road safety through the advancement of driving standards and implementation of the government's policies for improving the mechanical standards of vehicles.

nidirect.gov.uk/motoring

Contents

Introduction

Getting started

In this section, you'll learn about

- the requirements for your eyesight
- how to apply for your licence
- the 'Driver's Record' and official study aids
- finding and choosing a driving instructor
- practising without your instructor
- accompanying a learner driver.

Before you start

First things first

You've decided you want to learn to drive. This will give you the opportunity to learn a completely new skill, one that will open up a whole new world of independence. But driving also comes with responsibility – it's important that you know how to drive safely and responsibly, that you learn the skills and that you practise. The aim is that you become a safe driver – not just to pass the test, but for the rest of your life.

The first step is getting a provisional driving licence, but even before that you have to know that your eyesight is good enough to drive on the road.

Your eyesight

You **MUST** be able to read (with glasses or contact lenses, if necessary) a car number plate made after 1 September 2001 from 20 metres. If glasses or corrective lenses are required to read the number plate, they must be used whenever you're driving or riding.

You have to take an eyesight test at the start of your practical driving test. You must meet the legal requirement for eyesight, or you will not be allowed to continue with your test.

You must also meet the minimum eyesight standard for visual acuity and have an adequate field of vision. An optician can tell you about this and carry out tests if necessary. For more information on drivers' eyesight requirements, please see **www.gov.uk**

If you've had sight correction surgery, you should declare this when you apply for your provisional licence.

You're responsible for ensuring that your eyesight meets the minimum legal requirements every time you drive. The police can stop you at any time and ask you to take an eyesight test.

Number plates

Most cars on the road today have number plates like this one

AB69 DVL

area identifier age identifier random letters

11

Applying for your licence

You may apply for your first provisional licence when you're 15 years and 9 months old. You cannot start driving, though, until you're 17 years old. There is one exception. You can drive a car when you're 16 if you get, or have applied for, the enhanced rate of the mobility component of Personal Independence Payment (PIP).

Driving licences are issued by the Driver and Vehicle Licensing Agency (DVLA). You can apply online at **www.gov.uk**. Alternatively, you can apply by post. You can get an application form (D1) from certain post office branches or request one online at **www.gov.uk**

In Northern Ireland, the issuing authority is the Driver and Vehicle Agency (Licensing) (DVA) and the form is a DL1. For more information, see **nidirect.gov.uk/information-and-services/motoring/learners-and-new-drivers**

Send your completed form to the appropriate office (details are given on the form). Remember to include a passport-type photograph, as all provisional licences now issued are photocard licences. When you receive your provisional licence, check that all the details are correct. If you need to contact DVLA or DVA, you can do so via **www.gov.uk** and **nidirect.gov.uk/motoring**

Remember

You must have received your provisional driving licence before you start to drive on the road. This means that you must actually have it in your possession, not just have sent away for it.

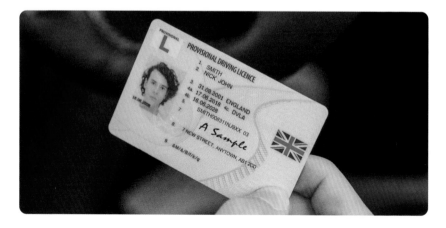

Structured learning

Learners who pass their driving test have had, on average, 40 to 50 hours of professional training combined with about 20 hours of private practice. This shows the importance of combining professional training and private practice while you're learning to drive.

To help you learn in a structured way, DVSA has produced a 'Driver's Record'.

The 'Driver's Record'

The 'Driver's Record' is a way of helping you and your driving instructor to keep a record of your progress while you're learning to drive. You can download a copy and take it with you to your driving lessons. See page 14 for details of how to do this.

Following a structured learning programme is beneficial to both you as a learner and your instructor. You need to learn the skill and then practise to get the experience.

You also need to learn both the theory and practical driving at the same time. This should help you to understand and apply the theory to actual driving.

The 'Driver's Record' contains a list of all the key skills that you need to achieve in order to become a safe driver and pass your test. It has space for you and your instructor to fill in as you progress through the various levels shown on the record.

You and your instructor will be able to see at a glance which topics you need to improve. Details of the key skills can be found on pages 24 to 100 of this book. Section 2 gives corresponding advice for an accompanying driver.

What are the 5 levels?

The meaning of each level is

1. Introduced – The subject is introduced and you're able to follow the instructions you're given

2. Helped – You're improving but still need a bit of help

3. Prompted – Sometimes you need prompting, especially if it's a new or unusual situation

4. Independent – You're dealing with this consistently, confidently and independently

5. Reflection – In conversation, you show that you understand how things would have been different if you had done something differently. You can adapt to situations and see why perfecting the skill makes you safer and more fuel efficient.

An important part of the structured learning process is practising what you've learnt during your lessons. Get together with your instructor and the person who will be helping you to practise, and discuss which areas you need to cover.

You can keep a record of any practice you have on different types of road and during different conditions between lessons on pages 208 to 209. You can also download this form from **www.gov.uk** or ask your instructor for a printed copy.

Fill these in when you go out with the person helping you to practise. You can also record any worries you may have about your driving and then discuss these with your instructor.

Keep this as a record of your 'Learning to Drive' experience.

Where can I get hold of a 'Driver's Record'?

If you have not got one, ask your instructor or download one by visiting **www.gov.uk**

Official study aids

Lessons and practice are the most important elements of learning to drive but, when you're not in the car, there are various books and electronic products to help you with all stages of driving – theory, hazard perception and practical.

The Official Highway Code Essential reading for all road users. This contains the rules of the road and the legislation that affects road users. It provides advice on road safety and best practice. 'The Official Highway Code' is updated from time to time, so make sure that you have a copy of the latest edition. As well as the print version, it's available as an eBook and an iPhone app. You can also find it online at **www.gov.uk**

DVSA also produces a series of books and electronic products to provide you with a sound knowledge of driving skills.

The Official DVSA Theory Test for Car Drivers Includes revision questions and answers for the multiple choice part of the theory test and explains why the answers are correct. If you're well prepared you will not find the questions difficult. This information is available

- as a book
- on DVD-ROM
- in app format
- online at DVSA learning zone
- as a digital download
- as an eBook.

You can buy official DVSA learning materials online at **safedrivingforlife.info/shop** or by calling our expert publications team on 0333 200 2401. The team can give you advice about learning materials and how to prepare for the tests and beyond. They can also help you select a suitable learning material if you have a special need; for example, if you have a learning disability or English is not your first language.

DVSA publications are also available from bookshops and online retailers. DVSA apps can be downloaded from the iOS App Store, Google Play store and Amazon Appstore and eBooks are available from your device's eBook store.

The Official DVSA Guide to Hazard Perception (DVD-ROM)
DVSA strongly recommends that you use this, preferably with your instructor, to prepare for the hazard perception part of the theory test. It's packed with useful tips, quizzes and expert advice. It also includes more than 100 interactive hazard perception clips, and your performance will receive a score so you'll know if you're ready to take the test.

The Official DVSA Theory Test for Car Drivers and The Official DVSA Guide to Hazard Perception are available individually or packaged together as The Official DVSA Complete Theory Test Kit, which provides all the learning materials for the theory test in one package.

The Official DVSA Theory Test Kit App The ideal way to prepare for your test on the go. The Theory Test Kit covers both the multiple choice and hazard perception parts of the test. Available from the iOS App Store and Google Play store.

The Official DVSA Theory Test for Car Drivers Online
This website provides you with instant access to all the latest DVSA theory test revision questions and answers. You can start revising straight away on whatever smartphone, tablet, laptop or computer you have. It's also packed with loads of helpful features so you get the most from your theory test revision. Simply choose the length of time that's right for you.
Go to **dvsalearningzone.co.uk/shop/car-theory-kit**

The Official DVSA Guide to Driving – the essential skills
This book is referenced in section 1 (key skills). It contains a wealth of information about driving skills, from the basic, helping you when you first start to drive, through to in-depth advice about dealing with various road and traffic conditions.

Choosing a driving instructor

If you're going to pay someone to teach you to drive, they must be an approved driving instructor (ADI) or hold a trainee licence.

DVSA is responsible for checking the instructional standards of ADIs. All ADIs must

- have held a full driving licence for at least 4 years
- pass a challenging theory and 2 practical tests
- reach and keep up a high standard of instruction. ADIs are regularly checked by DVSA
- be registered with DVSA
- display a green ADI licence on the windscreen of the vehicle during lessons.

It's unlikely that anyone except an ADI would have the experience, knowledge and training to teach you properly.

Trainee driving instructors have a trainee licence so that they can gain teaching experience before their qualifying examination. This licence is pink and must be displayed on the windscreen of the vehicle during lessons.

Finding an ADI

Ask friends or relatives for recommendations. Choose an instructor who has a good reputation. You can also ask them for their grade before starting a course of lessons.

What does each instructor grade mean?

The standard of instruction of all ADIs is checked regularly by DVSA. The instructor is then given a grade

A a high overall standard of instruction

B sufficient competence demonstrated.

ADI badge

Trainee ADI badge

Tip

Ask the ADI if they've signed up to the industry code of practice. This is a voluntary code that covers

- their level of qualification
- the personal conduct expected from them when giving tuition
- the professional conduct of their business
- the acceptability of their advertising
- their method of dealing with complaints.

An ADI will be able to help with all aspects of driving and advise you on

- what to study – DVSA produces a range of books, eBooks, DVD-ROMs, online materials and apps to help you learn to drive
- how to practise and what you should be practising
- when you're ready for your driving test
- further training after you've passed your test (see pages 187 to 189, which includes the Pass Plus scheme).

What if I find I do not like my instructor after I start lessons?

You can always find a new instructor.

It's important that you get on well with whoever is teaching you to drive. Different people prefer different teaching styles. You should try to find someone that suits you. It also helps if you feel comfortable with their car, as this will help to build your confidence.

Can I have lessons in my own car?

Some instructors are prepared to give you driving lessons in your own car. Ask about this when you first contact them, as some instructors will not do so for health and safety reasons.

For further information or advice, visit **www.gov.uk** or telephone DVSA on **0300 200 1122**.

Practising without your instructor

The more driving experience you get, the better. You need to gain experience on all types of road, including rural roads, and in different driving conditions. The more you practise and increase your experience, the more confident you'll become.

Your accompanying driver

The person helping you to practise must be at least 21 years old and have held a full EC/EEA licence for that type of vehicle for at least the last 3 years. Your accompanying driver cannot accept any payment for helping you practise.

The practice vehicle

Your practice vehicle must be roadworthy and properly insured for you to drive. It must also display L plates (or D plates in Wales) to the front and rear – make sure they're secure and do not obstruct your view.

If it helps, get together with both your instructor and the person who will be helping you to practise, so you can discuss what you need to do. Ask your instructor for advice on what skills you should practise after each lesson.

How to practise

Ask your accompanying driver to help you to practise

- on as many types of road as you can
- in all sorts of traffic and weather conditions, even in the dark
- on dual carriageways where the national speed limit applies. You may be asked to drive on this type of road during your test.

When you practise, your accompanying driver should make sure you

- avoid obstructing other traffic. Most drivers are tolerant of learners, but do not try their patience too much
- do not annoy local residents. For example, do not repeatedly practise emergency stops in the same quiet residential streets or practise on test routes
- do lots of general driving and do not simply practise the exercises included in the practical test.

Practising on motorways

Learner drivers can have driving lessons on motorways but only with an approved driving instructor (ADI) and in a car fitted with dual controls that's clearly displaying L plates.

Your ADI will be able to tell you when you're ready to take lessons on the motorway. This should be after you've had experience on a wide range of roads, and when you're just about ready to take your driving test. At this point, you should be a competent driver with an understanding of the theory of motorway driving.

Notes for the accompanying driver

Agreeing to accompany a learner is a responsibility not to be taken lightly. You'll be the person helping your learner get that important extra practice.

You must make sure that you have the right licence and that your car is insured for them to drive (see page 20). Your car will also need to display L plates (D plates in Wales) and have an additional interior mirror so that you can see what's happening behind.

When you accompany a learner, you're responsible for their actions. You'll need to stay calm and offer advice when needed. Have a chat with your learner and their instructor so that together you can decide what needs to be practised.

As the full licence-holder, you're responsible for the vehicle while supervising a learner. You cannot concentrate fully, watch out for danger or guide their actions safely while you're distracted; for example, by a phone conversation. You're breaking the law if you use your mobile phone or other hand-held device while you're supervising a learner driver.

Everyone learns at a different pace and finds different things difficult. Something that you find easy may be difficult for a learner. Be patient and constructive. Make sure that you're aware of the standard that's expected of a learner driver and the style of driving they're being taught. Some things may have changed since you learnt to drive and it can be confusing for the learner to receive different messages.

Section 2 of this book contains a lot more advice aimed at the accompanying driver, covering all of the key skills in addition to general hints and tips. Record your time spent in different situations on your 'Driver's Record'. This will help the 3 of you to work out where extra practice would be useful.

Learner drivers can have driving lessons on motorways, but only with a qualified approved driving instructor (ADI). See page 21.

Remember

You cannot receive payment for the time you spend helping your learner to practise.

The Official DVSA **Learning Zone**

www.dvsalearningzone.co.uk

Prepare to pass your theory test first time with The Official DVSA Theory Test Kit for Car Drivers Online, the only official online learning programme brought to you by DVSA, the people who set the tests.

It's part of The Official DVSA Learning Zone, and gives you access to all the latest DVSA theory test revision questions and answers, plus over 100 high-quality hazard perception clips. There's also a really helpful study section, so you get the most from your theory test revision.

You'll get

- All the latest DVSA theory test revision questions and answers
- Over 100 high-quality interactive hazard perception clips
- A helpful study section, with links to The Official Highway Code.

ve us a call on **01603 696860** or visit **www.dvsalearningzone.co.uk**

 @safedrivinglife safedrivinglife safe.driving.for.life safedrivingforlifeinfo

Section one

 **Key skills**

In this section, you'll learn about

- the references and how to find more information
- your legal responsibilities
- the techniques needed to pass your driving test
- ways to reflect on your driving.

Using this book

Use this book as a reference while you're learning to drive. It can also be used to keep a record of your progress.

The 'Driver's Record'

All the key skills from the 'Driver's Record' are shown on the following pages. On these pages, you'll find details of the standard you need to reach to become a safe driver in that skill and be fully prepared for your driving test.

As your instructor signs off the skill in your 'Driver's Record', make a note on the relevant page in this book.

Expert tips

As well as explaining the level that you need to achieve, this section includes useful tips from the people who set the tests. These have been drawn up from years of experience and from common mistakes made by candidates during their driving tests.

Recap questions

For each skill there are recap questions – try answering these to refresh your memory.

All the answers to the recap questions can be found in the books referred to at the foot of the relevant pages.

Reflection

Once you've reached the fourth level in all the key skills you should be driving confidently and safely. Sometimes

- you'll come across new situations
- your driving is not as good as it could be
- you'll make a mistake.

When this happens you should reflect on what happened and learn from it. The next time you come across a similar situation you'll be better prepared to cope with it. Reflection and learning is a process that should continue throughout your driving career.

How do I use the references?

Further information about each of the skills can be found by following the references at the foot of the relevant pages. The reference **HC** refers to 'The Official Highway Code' and the reference **DES** refers to 'The Official DVSA Guide to Driving – the essential skills'.

The **HC** references are prefixed with either the letter **r** or **p**. The letter **r** indicates the rule number and the letter **p** indicates the page number.

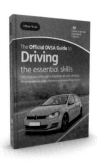

The **DES** references are prefixed with the letter **s**. This indicates the section of the book. See the example below.

References HC r245, p35 DES s2

Legal responsibilities

As a driver, it's your responsibility to know how the law relates to both yourself and your vehicle, so make sure that you're up to date with the rules and regulations.

To make sure you're in a fit condition to drive safely, you need to understand how the following affect you

- **health** – certain medical conditions must be reported to the Driver and Vehicle Licensing Agency (DVLA) (see **www.gov.uk** for details)
- **eyesight** – can you read a car number plate from 20 metres? If you need glasses to read it, then you must always wear them when you're driving (see page 11)
- **drink** – do not drink and drive. There's a legal limit but it's safer not to drink at all if you're going to drive
- **drugs** – never take drugs before driving; the effects can be more severe than those caused by alcohol. Even some over-the-counter drugs can make you drowsy
- **tiredness** – if you're tired, you're more likely to have a collision. On a long journey, have a break every 2 hours or so
- **mobile phones** – it's illegal to use a hand-held phone while driving. Even a hands-free phone can distract you while you're driving.

To make sure the car you're driving complies with the regulations, you must check that

- the vehicle is taxed and has an MOT certificate if it needs one (see **www.gov.uk** for details)
- the vehicle is insured for you to drive
- the vehicle is in a roadworthy condition.

You must make sure you have a licence for the category of vehicle you're going to drive.

L plates should be clearly displayed on the front and back of the vehicle you're driving (D plates can be used in Wales). These can be bought from the Safe Driving for Life website at **safedrivingforlife.info/shop/product/ official-dvsa-magnetic-l-plates**

Remember

You need to know the traffic rules and regulations – these can be found in The Highway Code.

Who can teach me to drive?

Anyone can teach you to drive but they must be at least 21 years old and have held a full EC/EEA licence for that type of vehicle for at least the last 3 years. However, only ADIs and trainee licence-holders can teach for payment. They must display their licence badge on the windscreen during lessons. It's unlikely that anyone who is not an ADI will have the skills and knowledge to teach you to the standard required to pass your driving test.

Tips from the experts

Make sure that you know what to do if you're involved in a road traffic incident. As well as dealing with the scene of the incident, you may need to report it to the police.

HC r281–287

Distraction

Using a mobile phone while you're driving is illegal because of the distraction it causes. Even a hands-free phone can distract you while you're driving. The best advice is to switch it off when you're driving, otherwise you might be tempted to look at it if it rings or alerts you to a text message. Stop safely before checking your phone or reading any messages.

The rules about mobile phones also apply to the person accompanying you while you practise.

What to expect on your driving test

You'll be asked about legal responsibilities during your theory test.

You'll need to show your driving licence and pass the eyesight test before starting your practical driving test.

Recap questions

Q1 What are the legal requirements for someone helping a learner to drive?

Q2 What's the first thing you should do if you're involved in a road traffic incident?

Reflection

Do you know about the New Drivers Act? How would you feel if you were caught breaking the law and lost your driving licence?

Accompanying driver advice p118

More information is available here HC most of the code DES s2

29

Safety checks

It's important that your car is in good working order before you start the engine. You need to be aware of what to check, how to do it and how often to do it.

You need to carry out appropriate safety checks on your car and know about

- **F**uel – whether you have enough fuel for your journey and, if necessary, plan where to refuel your car
- **L**ights – check all lights are clean and working
- **O**il – where and how to check the levels of engine oil and brake fluid
- **W**ater – and other fluids, including screenwash and coolant – where they are and how to check them
- **E**lectrics – battery and charging system, indicators, horn and other warning devices – check they're in good working order
- **R**ubber – the correct pressure for your tyres, how to measure it and how to check tread depth and tyre condition.

Remember

Fuel, Lights, Oil, Water, Electrics, Rubber. Just think **FLOWER**, then you should not have any problems remembering your checks.

Also, you need to know how to check that the brakes and steering are working properly before you start to drive.

Understand the importance of good maintenance

To do this, you need to know about

- daily and weekly vehicle checks and how frequently they should be made
- when your car requires professional maintenance, including the correct service intervals for your car
- what checks to make before starting a journey, especially longer ones
- how to clear and clean your windscreen so you have the best visibility at all times.

Can I check all this myself?

You'll need someone to help you check the brake lights. It's also easier and quicker to check the other lights if someone checks them while you're working the controls.

What kind of safety question will I be asked?

There are a limited number of safety-check questions that you can be asked during your driving test. They will mostly take the form of 'show me' or 'tell me' questions and will relate to the subjects detailed on this page. See annex 2 on page 210 for all the official safety-check questions.

Tips from the experts

Make sure that you're familiar with the car you're driving, and that you can explain or demonstrate how you would carry out simple safety checks on that car.

You'll need to open the bonnet to carry out some of the checks – make sure that you know how to open the bonnet and also that you shut it properly once you've carried out the checks.

Regular servicing will keep the engine running efficiently and save you money in the long run.

What to expect on your driving test

Your examiner will ask you

- one 'tell me' question at the beginning of your test, before you start driving. This is where you explain how you'd carry out a safety task
- one 'show me' question while you're driving; for example, showing how to wash the windscreen using the car controls.

Check out these DVSA videos about the 'show me, tell me' questions:

https://www.youtube.com/watch?v=damj01nXcZU

https://www.youtube.com/watch?v=uh8slnP76-w

Recap question

Q1   What's the minimum tread depth for your car tyres?

Reflection

Do you miss out routinely checking the car? If you do, ask yourself what would make you regret missing one of those vital checks. Did you know that running out of fuel is the single biggest cause of breakdowns on the motorway?

Accompanying driver advice p120

More information is available here HC r89, 97, p128 DES s5, 14

Cockpit checks

These checks may be simple, but they're essential. The car you're using needs to be comfortable and ready for you to drive before you start the engine.

You need to check

- all doors are closed properly and the parking brake is on
- your seat is in the correct position and you can reach the foot controls comfortably – if you have to adjust it, make sure it locks. Also make sure the head restraint is properly adjusted to give protection against whiplash injuries
- the steering wheel should be adjusted so that you can use it easily
- your seat belt is fastened, adjusted correctly and comfortable*
- the mirrors are correctly adjusted – make sure that you check the interior and exterior mirrors so that you have the best view
- the parking brake again and check that the gear lever is in neutral (if you're driving an automatic, that the gear lever is in P or N)
- whether you'll need to refuel your car.

You need to know

- the correct order in which to carry out the cockpit checks – you need to make sure that you're seated comfortably before you adjust your mirrors
- the various ways that you can adjust your seat to give you the best driving position
- how to adjust your mirrors, including adjusting the interior mirror so that you're not dazzled by the driver behind you at night.

Remember

It's against the law to drive without your seat belt fastened unless you have a medical exemption from having to wear a seat belt.* The driver is also responsible for making sure that any child under 14 who travels in their car wears a seat belt.

*If an inertia-reel seat belt has temporarily locked, because the vehicle is parked on a gradient, the driver may move the vehicle. As soon as the mechanism has released itself, the driver **MUST** stop and fasten their seat belt.

Can I readjust anything while I'm driving?

If you need to readjust your mirrors (apart from setting the interior mirror to its anti-dazzle position), seat position or steering wheel, find a safe place to stop before making any adjustments.

Do I need to do these checks every time?

Get into the habit of doing these checks every time – it's particularly important if other people use the car.

Tips from the experts

Make sure that you do these checks, in the right order, before you start the engine. This is particularly important if you're not the only person using the car.

What to expect on your driving test

Your examiner will watch to make sure that you carry out all the checks, in the right order. Before you start the engine, make sure the gear lever is in neutral and the parking brake is on.

Leaving the car

When you've safely parked the car and stopped the engine, you'll need to open the door safely. Use your mirrors and look around because you must make sure you do not hit anyone with your door.

Recap questions

Q1 Is it the responsibility of the driver to make sure that adult passengers wear seat belts?

Q2 What could be a consequence of failing to carry out the cockpit checks properly?

Q3 Why should you check that the head restraint is in the correct position?

Tip

If you get into the habit of reaching for the door handle with your left hand, you'll be better able to see anything approaching from behind your car and **reduce the risk to vulnerable road users**. In windy conditions, it will also help you to stop the door suddenly being blown wide open.

Reflection

Do you find yourself needing to adjust anything after you've started driving? If so, ask yourself, 'Why didn't I check and adjust this before I started driving?' or, 'What might happen if I'm involved in an incident because of this?'

Accompanying driver advice p122

More information is available here HC r97, 99 DES s3–5

Controls and instruments

You need to concentrate on what's happening around you when you're driving, so operating the vehicle's controls should become second nature.

You need to be able to operate the controls safely and confidently without looking at them. This includes the

- **foot controls** – the accelerator, clutch and footbrake pedals
- **hand controls** – the parking brake, steering wheel, indicators, headlights and gearstick
- **other controls** – the horn (you need to know when and for what reason you can legally use the horn), windscreen wipers, demister and heated windows. You also need to be aware of any controls specific to the car you're driving.

You need to know the meaning and function of each element of the instrument panel.

Can I look at the gear lever?

If the car is moving, you should not take your eyes off the road to look at the gear lever.

Do not coast with the gear lever in neutral or the clutch pedal down.

Should I steer and change gear at the same time?

For maximum control, you need both hands to steer. Try to change to the appropriate gear before starting to turn.

Tips from the experts

Make sure you're familiar with all the hand- and foot-operated controls before you start driving the car. You should be able to reach and operate all the controls while you're driving and without having to take your eyes off the road to find them.

On vehicles with manual transmission, there are 3 foot-operated controls: the accelerator, brake and clutch pedals. These controls should be used smoothly when moving off, accelerating, slowing and stopping. Harsh use of these controls will use more fuel than if they're used smoothly.

If you're driving a vehicle with automatic transmission, there will only be 2 foot-operated controls: the accelerator and the brake pedal.

Tip

To give yourself time to use the controls smoothly, look well ahead while you're driving. The earlier you see and start to respond to a hazard, the more time you'll have to respond smoothly and safely. Driving in this way can also save you fuel.

What to expect on your driving test

Your examiner will want to see that you can

- demonstrate good control of the vehicle throughout your driving test
- show an understanding of the vehicle's instruments.

Recap question

Q1   When is it illegal to use your horn?

Reflection

Do you often find yourself needing to brake hard? If you do, ask yourself whether you could have predicted the need to brake and simply eased off the accelerator a bit earlier? Smooth use of the controls can lead to a significant fuel saving.

Accompanying driver advice p124

More information is available here HC r110 DES s3

Moving away and stopping

You have to move away and stop every time you drive and that's why it's so important to make sure that you know how to move away and stop safely.

To do this, you need to

- be able to move away and stop safely on level ground, on a hill, at an angle and straight ahead
- use the MSM and PSL routines (see below)
- observe what's happening around you and be aware of any blind spots (see page 44)
- co-ordinate your use of the accelerator, clutch and footbrake so that you move off and slow down safely and smoothly
- be able to use the parking brake and steering competently
- know where and when to look, what to look for and how to act safely on what you see
- be able to identify suitable stopping places
- know where and when to signal.

Remember

The MSM and PSL routines are key to virtually all aspects of driving.

Mirrors – Signal – Manoeuvre

M – Use your **mirrors** to check the position of traffic around and behind you

S – **Signal** when necessary and in good time so that others know what you intend to do

M – A **manoeuvre** involves a change in position and/or speed.

Position – Speed – Look

P – Position your car correctly for the move you want to make

S – Adjust your speed so it's appropriate for the manoeuvre

L – Have a final look to check it's safe before you start to steer.

What if I do not have a clear view of the road?

If you cannot see because someone has parked close to you, edge out slowly and only move off when you can see it's safe.

How do I stop if someone is following very closely?

Make sure that you signal in good time to let them know that you're going to slow down and stop.

Tips from the experts

Always use your mirrors but only signal if you need to – do not just signal automatically.

Check your blind spots (see page 44). Do not move away without looking and do not make anyone else stop or swerve.

Move away smoothly, in the correct gear and do not accelerate excessively.

What to expect on your driving test

Your examiner will ask you to stop at the side of the road and then move away again.

Every time you perform either of these manoeuvres, the examiner will watch your

- use of the controls and MSM routine each time you stop and then move off – do not forget to incorporate the PSL routine when you're stopping
- observation of, and safe responses to, other road users
- judgement in selecting a safe and suitable place to stop.

You may need to check your blind spot more than once when moving off from behind another car.

Recap questions

Q1 When would you not need to signal before moving away?

Q2 What are you looking for in a safe place to stop?

Reflection

Have you ever moved away into the path of another vehicle or stopped without first checking what was behind you? If you have, ask yourself why that happened and what you could do to make sure it does not happen again.

Accompanying driver advice p126

More information is available here HC r103, 159–161, 238–252 DES s5

Safe positioning

Make sure that you drive in the correct position for the road on which you're travelling. It's important not only for your safety but also for the safety of other road users.

You should be able to

- use the MSM and PSL routines (see pages 38 to 39)
- show good lane discipline. Plan ahead and make sure that you move into the correct lane in good time
- adapt your road position to suit the road width and traffic conditions
- keep a safe position during normal driving, especially around bends
- take up the correct position on a one-way street.

To respond to the positions of other road users, you must understand

- how other vehicles, such as lorries and cyclists, need to position themselves
- what clearance you need to leave when passing stationary vehicles, cyclists or obstructions.

Remember

Plan ahead and make sure you move into the correct lane in good time. Do not be late changing lanes.

How much room should I give a cyclist when overtaking?

Give them plenty of room – as much room as you would give a car. They may have to move away from the kerb in order to avoid something you cannot see.

What if there are no markings on the road?

Position your vehicle sensibly even if there are no road markings. Do not drive too close to the kerb or too close to the centre of the road.

Always leave plenty of room when passing a parked car, in case a door opens suddenly!

Tips from the experts

Do not obstruct other road users by being in the wrong lane, straddling lanes or swapping lanes unnecessarily.

At roundabouts, do not cut across the path of other vehicles.

Make sure everyone around you knows where you want to go.

What to expect on your driving test

Your examiner will watch to make sure that you

- are using the MSM and PSL routines and acting on what you've seen
- respond to signs and road markings by selecting the correct lane in good time
- keep a safe position for the situation.

Recap questions

Q1 When should you use the right-hand lane of a dual carriageway?

Q2 A large vehicle is emerging from a junction on the right. How might this affect your positioning?

Q3 Why is it important to move into the correct lane as soon as you can?

Reflection

Have you ever found yourself in the wrong lane? Why was that and what could you do to prevent it happening?

Accompanying driver advice p128

More information is available here HC r127–146, 152–156 DES s7, 8

43

Mirrors – vision and use

You must know what's happening around you at all times and act safely on what you see.

You must know

- how to make use of the MSM and PSL routines (see pages 38 to 39)
- when to use the mirrors
- why you need to use the mirrors and the importance of regular mirror checks
- how to act on what you see in your mirrors.

You need to know about the different mirrors fitted to your vehicle and

- the uses for the interior mirror and the 2 exterior mirrors
- the effect that flat, concave and convex mirrors have, and how you interpret what you see in them
- what areas each mirror covers and where the blind spots are.

How do I check my blind spots when I'm moving?

It's dangerous to turn and look all the way around while you're driving, as you may lose touch with what's happening in front, but you can give a quick sideways glance.

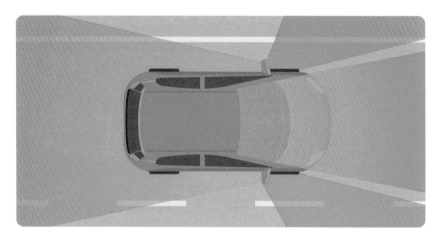

There are blind spots between what you can see when looking forward and what you can see in your mirrors. The car's bodywork also creates blind spots that can hide smaller road users.

Which mirror should I look in first?

Normally you should look in the interior mirror first, followed by the exterior mirrors if necessary. Use of the exterior mirrors will depend on the situation.

Tips from the experts

Always check your mirrors before you signal and remember, the situation may not always require a signal. Act sensibly on what you see and think about how your actions might affect other road users near you.

Use all of your mirrors periodically while you drive, especially as you approach any hazard, so that you're constantly aware of what's happening around you.

Make sure that you always use your mirrors before

- moving off
- signalling
- turning left or right
- changing lanes or overtaking
- changing speed or stopping
- opening your car door.

What to expect on your driving test

Your examiner will watch to make sure that you're aware of the scene all around, so you need to make sure that you use your mirrors and act safely on what you see.

Recap question

Q1   What are the advantages and disadvantages of convex mirrors?

Reflection

Have you ever been surprised by a vehicle that you did not see coming up behind you? Why was that? Could you do anything to make sure you're better prepared?

Remember to make sure your mirrors are correctly adjusted before you start driving.

Accompanying driver advice p130

More information is available here HC r161 DES s4

Signals

You need to understand, and respond safely to, signals given by other motorists and give clear, well-timed signals to other road users so that they know what you're planning to do.

You need to know

- why it's necessary to give signals – you need to signal to let others know what you intend to do
- when and how to give signals (it's important that you time your signal to allow others to respond safely)
- when and how to give arm signals
- when signals are not required.

To understand signals given by other people using the road, you need to know

- the significance of other types of signal, including brake, reversing and hazard warning lights
- how to read signals given by traffic controllers such as school crossing patrols.

Remember

You should only use signals that are shown in The Highway Code.

Should I always signal?

If you have a clear view and can see there's no-one who will benefit from your signal, there's no reason to signal.

Could I signal too early?

It could be confusing to signal too early – for example, if there are several side roads close together. Think about the situation before you give a signal.

1 Reversing light

Shows a vehicle is about to reverse or is reversing. When you're reversing, it helps you to see what's behind you in the dark.

2 Rear/brake light

Brake lights can often be an early warning of what's happening further down the road.

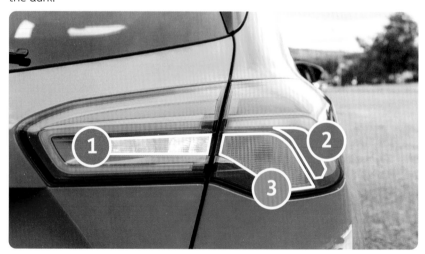

3 Indicator light

Indicators normally show a change of direction. Both indicators flashing may mean a vehicle is stopped ahead.

Fog light

In seriously reduced visibility, rear fog lights can help to make vehicles easier to see. They are often mounted lower down on the car bodywork.

Tips from the experts

Do not be tempted to flash your headlights for any other reason than that given in The Highway Code.

Always make sure to cancel your signal after you've carried out a manoeuvre. Leaving a signal on can lead to dangerous situations because other road users may take action based on the direction they expect you to go.

What to expect on your driving test

The examiner will expect well-timed signals and safe responses to signals from others.

Recap questions

Q1 When can you flash your headlights?

Q2 In what kind of situation would you not have to signal?

Reflection

Have you ever failed to cancel a signal, or forgotten to give one – for example to leave a roundabout? How does it make you feel when other people do that? What could you do to improve your signalling skills in the future?

Accompanying driver advice p132

More information is available here HC r103–112, 116, p102 DES s5, 10

Anticipation and planning

These skills are found in all areas of driving. You should always be aware of what's going on around you while planning what you need to do in response. Planning ahead can also save you fuel, because easing off the accelerator earlier means you may not need to use the brakes as often or as heavily.

You need to be able to

- use the MSM and PSL routines (see pages 38 to 39)
- identify hazards from clues and respond to them in good time
- recognise times, places and conditions that mean there's a higher risk. This includes weather conditions
- use scanning techniques to enable you to plan ahead so that you can prioritise how you'll deal with hazards you encounter.

To anticipate the actions of others, you need to be familiar with the risks associated with the various types of road user

- **cyclists** – give cyclists room and take special care when you cross cycle lanes. In traffic queues, watch out for cyclists passing on your left
- **motorcyclists** – look for them, especially at junctions and in slow-moving traffic
- **drivers of large vehicles** – they may need to take up different or unusual road positions; for example, when turning at some junctions or roundabouts
- **pedestrians** – take special care with the very young, older people and those with disabilities. They may not have seen you and could step out suddenly
- **animals** – give horse riders as much room as possible and pass them slowly
- **emergency vehicles** – do not panic, check where they're coming from and try to keep out of their way. If necessary, pull in to the side of the road and stop.

Can I use my hazard warning lights while I'm moving?

Yes, you can use them to warn other drivers of a hazard or an obstruction ahead, but only when you're driving on a motorway or unrestricted dual carriageway. On all other roads, you must only use these lights when your vehicle is stationary.

What do I gain from anticipating and planning?

If you scan ahead, you should be able to anticipate potentially hazardous situations. By being prepared, you can deal with situations more easily, safely and in a controlled way.

Tips from the experts

You need to be constantly checking what's going on in front, behind and around you. Planning ahead reduces the risk of something happening where you have to react suddenly.

Take every opportunity to look for clues; for example, reflections in windows or seeing a pedestrian's feet on the far side of a parked vehicle. Such clues can help you anticipate what's likely to happen next.

What to expect on your driving test

You'll be expected to be aware of other road users and road and weather conditions at all times. You'll also need to show an awareness of the hazards they present and respond safely and in good time.

Recap questions

Q1 What hazards could you come across on a busy residential street?

Q2 Why might a motorcyclist need to swerve suddenly?

Reflection

Has anything happened that caused you to react suddenly? How did this make you feel? Could you have anticipated it happening and taken action earlier? What clues did you miss?

If a cyclist looks over their shoulder, hold back; they may be about to turn or move out across your path.

Accompanying driver advice p134

More information is available here HC r146, 160–161, 204–237 DES s7, 10

Use of speed

Your speed should be based on various factors, including the condition of the road, weather and traffic, and the presence of pedestrians. Always drive within the speed limit.

You need to

- know the national speed limits and restrictions for different types of vehicle and any restricted speed limits for the road you're on
- adjust your speed to take account of road, weather and traffic conditions
- choose the appropriate speed where there are pedestrians and in traffic-calmed areas
- know the stopping distance for your vehicle in different conditions and how to calculate a safe separation distance between yourself and the vehicle in front.

Remember

Speed limits do not mean that you have to drive at that speed. Use your judgement and drive at a speed that's within the speed limit and that suits the conditions.

Can I exceed the speed limit to overtake someone?

No, you must always stay within the speed limit. It's illegal to break it, even for a short period of time.

Can I drive too slowly?

You should drive confidently and at a reasonable speed. If you drive too slowly or hesitate unnecessarily, it can be very frustrating for other drivers and this can lead to road traffic incidents.

Never drive faster than the speed limit – safety cameras are there to make sure everyone stays within the speed limit.

Tips from the experts

Do not drive too fast for the road and traffic conditions and make sure that you can stop safely, well within the distance you can see to be clear. Leave extra distance for stopping on wet or slippery roads.

Do not change speed unpredictably.

Learn how to control your vehicle's speed as you approach junctions. Avoid being over-cautious – for example, by stopping and waiting when it's safe to continue.

What to expect on your driving test

Your examiner will watch how you control your vehicle's speed throughout your test.

They'll want to see that you can

- make reasonable progress along the road and respond to changing conditions
- keep up with other traffic but comply with the speed limits
- show confidence, together with sound judgement.

Recap questions

Q1 What's the national speed limit for cars on a dual carriageway?

Q2 What separation distance should you leave between you and the vehicle in front on a wet road?

Reflection

Have you ever found yourself driving faster than you realised? Excessive speed is a major factor in road incidents. How can you be more aware of and stay within speed limits?

Accompanying driver advice p136

More information is available here HC r124–126, p42–43 DES s7, 10

Other traffic

In most cases when you're driving, there will be other traffic on the road. You need to be able to deal safely and confidently when meeting, crossing and overtaking other vehicles.

You need to be able to deal with

- **meeting** – where there are parked cars or obstructions on your side of the road, you must be prepared to give way to oncoming traffic. On narrow roads, you may need to use passing places
- **crossing** – you normally need to cross the path of other traffic if you're turning right into a side road or driveway. Make sure that you position your car correctly, as close to the centre of the road as is safe, and watch out for oncoming traffic, stopping if necessary. Do not forget to check your mirror before turning, in case a vehicle overtakes you while you're waiting to turn
- **overtaking** – overtake only if you can do so legally and safely. Check the speed and position of any vehicles behind (they might be planning to overtake you), in front, and coming towards you before you decide to overtake.

You need to know

- the MSM and PSL routines (see pages 38 to 39)
- why and when to give way – you should not cause another road user to slow down or alter their course when they have priority
- the significance of passing places, warning signs, road markings and how to deal with obstructions
- the importance of planning and anticipation, and acting safely on what you see
- how to drive on all road types, including a one-way or two-way road, a three-lane two-way road, a dual carriageway and a motorway.

Remember

Do not overtake as you approach a junction. A vehicle may pull out of the junction into your path.

If a driver is indicating, can I pull out before they turn?

Always wait until you're sure they're turning before you move out. They may have forgotten to cancel their signal from an earlier manoeuvre.

Can I flash my lights to give someone the go-ahead?

No. The Highway Code states that you should only flash your lights as a warning, to let someone know you're there.

Tips from the experts

When passing parked cars, watch out for doors opening, pedestrians (especially children) stepping out from between the cars, and vehicles pulling out.

When overtaking cyclists or horse riders, slow right down and give them as much room as you would for a car.

If you're going to pass an obstruction or overtake, start planning early so that you get a better view of the road ahead.

What to expect on your driving test

Your examiner will watch to see how you

- apply the MSM and PSL routines
- respond to road and traffic conditions
- handle the car's controls.

Recap questions

Q1   Give 3 examples of where it's against the law to overtake

Q2   On which side can you pass traffic if you're driving on a one-way road?

Q3   You see a car coming towards you on a narrow road. There's a passing place just ahead on the other side of the road. What should you do?

Reflection

Have you ever been frustrated by following a slow-moving vehicle? What could you do to make the delay less stressful?

If there's an obstruction on your side of the road, plan ahead so that you can give way to oncoming traffic.

Accompanying driver advice p139

More information is available here HC r133–143, 146, 151–155, 162–168 DES s7, 8, 10

Junctions

There are many different types of junction. You need to be able to negotiate any junction on any type of road safely, without holding up other traffic unnecessarily.

You need to deal safely and confidently with all types of junction, including

- **T-junctions and Y-junctions** – you need to make sure that you position yourself so that you get the best view of the road into which you're turning
- **crossroads** – always check who has priority as you approach a crossroads and be aware of the movement of any other traffic
- **slip roads** – these are there to help you match your speed to that of the traffic on the main road
- **unmarked junctions** – be cautious as no-one has priority here
- **junctions on all types of road** – urban and rural roads, dual carriageways and one-way streets.

You need to know the

- MSM and PSL routines (see pages 38 to 39)
- rules for turning at, entering into and emerging from a junction. These include the need to position your car correctly, adjust your speed and stop if necessary
- ways other road users turn right at crossroads and know how to adapt to different situations
- significance of advance warning signs and road markings, and acting correctly on what you see
- rules of priority, especially when dealing with unmarked junctions
- importance of good observation.

Remember

You need to look both ways when you're turning left – there may be another vehicle on your side of the road.

What if a pedestrian is crossing the road that I'm turning into?

You should be checking as you approach the turning. A pedestrian who has already started to cross has priority, so give way. Remember, they might not have seen you.

How can I improve my view of the road that I'm turning into?

Sometimes buildings, hedges, bends in the road or parked cars can obscure your view. Edge forward slowly until you can see the road clearly before you pull out.

Tips from the experts

In a one-way street, move into the correct lane as soon as you can do so safely.

When approaching a junction, make sure that you slow down in good time so that you do not have to brake heavily if you need to stop.

Watch out for pedestrians, cyclists and motorcyclists when you're turning, as they're not as easy to see as larger vehicles.

What to expect on your driving test

Your examiner will watch carefully to take account of your

- use of the MSM and PSL routines
- position and speed as you approach junctions
- observation and judgement.

Recap questions

Q1 When can you wait on the yellow crisscross lines at a box junction?

Q2 Who has priority if there are no road markings at a crossroads?

Q3 How should you negotiate a traffic-light-controlled junction that has an advanced stop line for cyclists?

Reflection

Many collisions happen at road junctions and 'I did not see you' is often mentioned. Why do you think that is? Is there anything you could do to reduce the risk at junctions?

Usually, when emerging from a junction, you should keep well to the left if you're turning left. If you're turning right, keep as close to the centre of the road as is safe.

Accompanying driver advice p142

More information is available here HC r170–183 DES s8

Roundabouts

To deal with roundabouts safely and confidently, you should have a thorough understanding of the rules that apply when approaching and negotiating them.

You need to be able to safely negotiate different types of roundabout, including

- **standard roundabouts** – you should know how to approach and negotiate roundabouts even when there are no road markings directing you into particular lanes
- **mini-roundabouts** – you'll probably need to adjust your speed on approach because there's less room to manoeuvre and less time to signal
- **multiple and satellite roundabouts** – assess the layout of the roundabouts by looking at the signs on approach. Treat each roundabout separately and apply the normal rules
- **traffic-light-controlled roundabouts** – priorities will often be different from normal roundabouts here.

You need to know

- how and when to apply the MSM and PSL routines (see pages 38 to 39)
- the importance of effective observation and awareness of the traffic around you
- how to position your car correctly and which lane to use, both as you approach and when you're on a roundabout
- who has priority when you're entering a roundabout
- the procedure for leaving a roundabout.

Remember

If you're in a queue, do not move forward before checking that the vehicle in front of you is moving. They may judge the situation differently.

What if there's a long vehicle at the roundabout?

Stay well back and give it plenty of room. It might need to take a different course as it approaches and goes around the roundabout.

When should I start indicating to show I'm taking an exit?

You need to turn your left indicator on just after you've passed the exit before the one that you want to take. If your signal does not cancel automatically, cancel it manually when you've finished turning.

Tips from the experts

Approach the roundabout at the correct speed so that you can assess other traffic using the roundabout. If you need to stop, avoid braking harshly.

Roundabouts are there to help traffic move freely. Do not stop unless you need to.

Look at all the road signs and markings and make sure you get into the correct lane in good time.

What to expect on your driving test

Your examiner will take account of your ability to deal with roundabouts without undue hesitation. This will include your use of the MSM and PSL routines, your position, speed on approach, observation and judgement throughout.

Recap question

Q1   Why would a cyclist signal right but stay in the left-hand lane as they approach a roundabout?

Reflection

Some people find roundabouts difficult to deal with. Have you ever become confused and taken the wrong exit? How could you make sure you're better prepared?

Accompanying driver advice p145

More information is available here HC r184–190 DES s8

Pedestrian crossings

You should be aware of the basic rules that apply to all pedestrian crossings but you also need to know the differences between each type of crossing.

You need to safely negotiate different types of crossing. This includes

- **crossings controlled by lights** – pelican, puffin and toucan crossings
- **zebra crossings** – which have no lights controlling them
- **school crossing patrols** – these are not always at marked crossings
- **split crossings** – this includes crossings that are staggered and those that have a central refuge.

You need to know

- the importance of effective scanning as you approach a crossing
- how to recognise the different types of crossing from their visual characteristics
- how you should apply the MSM and PSL routines (see pages 38 to 39)
- the correct speed at which to approach the crossings and the rules concerning overtaking and parking near crossings
- when you need to stop for pedestrians who are waiting to cross
- the times and places where there's likely to be high risk; for example, near schools
- the effect that different weather conditions have on your ability to see and stop safely.

 Remember

It's illegal to park on a crossing or on the zigzag lines on either side of the crossing. It's also illegal to overtake the vehicle nearest the crossing.

Can I wave to let a pedestrian know they can cross?

You should never wave pedestrians across in front of you as you could lead them into danger. Let them decide for themselves when it's safe to cross.

What should I look for when I'm approaching a crossing?

Watch out for pedestrians walking close to crossings, especially zebra crossings, as they may start to cross without looking for traffic.

Tips from the experts

Make sure that you approach all crossings at a speed that allows you to stop safely if you need to.

As you approach a zebra crossing, look for pedestrians who may be intending to use the crossing.

Be patient when you're waiting at a crossing. Do not try to hurry those who are crossing by revving your engine, sounding your horn or edging forward.

What to expect on your driving test

Your examiner will watch carefully to assess how you deal with pedestrian crossings during your test. This includes how you prepare on the approach to crossings even when you do not have to stop to let pedestrians cross.

Recap questions

Q1 Which type of crossing has a flashing amber phase, and what does it mean for you as a driver?

Q2 What do the zigzag lines at a crossing mean?

Reflection

Why might you fail to notice someone waiting at a zebra crossing? What could you do to raise your awareness of pedestrian crossings?

If you're waiting in a queue of traffic, do not straddle a crossing. Hold back, as someone may want to cross before you're able to move off. At a controlled crossing, the lights might change.

Accompanying driver advice p147

More information is available here HC r191–199 DES s7

Reversing

You should be able to reverse smoothly and safely while under complete control. This includes reversing to the left and right around sweeping curves and sharp corners.

You need to be confident reversing

- around a left and a right corner – including square and gently curved corners as well as on the straight
- on a level road and on a gradient
- on a narrow or wide road
- on a flat road or one with a camber
- on the left- and right-hand sides of the road
- into driveways
- into and out of parking spaces (see pages 78 to 80).

You should know how to

- reverse accurately
- co-ordinate your hand and foot controls so that your vehicle moves smoothly
- steer in the correct manner
- make use of effective all-round observation throughout the time you're reversing
- reverse without undue delay
- take account of the way the car moves when you're reversing.

Remember

You can undo your seat belt while you're reversing if it interferes with your driving. Do not forget to do it up again before driving away.

Where should I look when I'm reversing?

Look mainly out of the back window, but do not forget to check all around throughout the time you're reversing and particularly at the point you start to turn.

What should I do if I cannot see clearly behind?

Get someone to guide you if you cannot see clearly.

Tips from the experts

As you reverse, keep a good lookout for traffic and especially vulnerable road users, such as cyclists and pedestrians. Remember, children can easily be hidden from view.

Reverse sensors and reversing cameras are useful driving aids. If you have them fitted, you should combine using the technology with good observation – you may see a situation developing before the sensors have detected it.

What to expect on your driving test

Your examiner will ask you to carry out one exercise using reverse gear. It may be the 'stop on the right-hand side of the road' manoeuvre or a reverse parking exercise (see pages 78 to 80). For the 'stop on the right-hand side of the road' manoeuvre, you'll be asked to stop on the right-hand side of the road, reverse for 2 car lengths and rejoin the traffic (see diagram).

Your examiner will watch to make sure that you reverse under full control, keeping reasonably close to the kerb. They'll assess your observation and how you respond to other road users.

Recap questions

Q1 How would other road users know that you intend to reverse?

Q2 Into what type of road should you not reverse?

Reflection

Have you ever relied entirely on your door mirrors while you were reversing? Have you become so focused on the mirror that you forgot to check around? What could you do to improve your awareness?

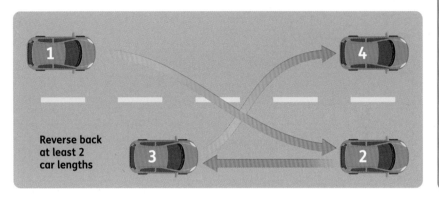

The 'stop on the right-hand side of the road' manoeuvre. Follow the steps from 1 to 4.

Accompanying driver advice p148

More information is available here HC r200–203 DES s9

Turning the vehicle around

To turn your vehicle around, it's often easiest and safest to use a roundabout or reverse into a side street. However, if these options are not available, you may need to turn your vehicle around in the road.

You need to be able to turn your vehicle around

- on a flat road or one with a camber
- under full control
- accurately judging the width of the road
- while looking for and responding to other road users
- without running into or mounting either kerb.

You should know how to

- observe carefully all around throughout the manoeuvre, especially checking your blind spots
- respond safely to other road users
- co-ordinate the hand and foot controls so that your vehicle moves smoothly
- steer in the correct manner while turning as tightly as possible.

Remember

Always start to turn your wheels in the opposite direction just before you stop. Do not steer while the car is stationary – this is called dry steering and can damage your tyres and steering.

What if the road is narrow?

Depending on the width of the road, how difficult your vehicle is to steer and the length of your vehicle, you may need to move forward and backwards several times to complete the turn.

Do I need to use the parking brake?

You may need to use the parking brake to prevent the car from rolling forward or backward if there's a pronounced camber or slope on the road.

Tips from the experts

Check the road is clear in both directions before you start to move across.

The key is to keep the vehicle moving slowly while steering briskly.

What to expect on your driving test

This manoeuvre is tested only on driving tests taken in Northern Ireland. However, your instructor should still teach you how to turn the car around; it's a valuable skill you will need throughout your driving career.

Recap question

Q1 What might you damage on your car if you turn the steering wheel while the car is stationary?

Reflection

What could happen if you try and turn your car around on a busy road? Why is this an example of bad driving?

Accompanying driver advice **p150**

More information is available here **HC r200 DES s9**

Country roads

Country roads vary from trunk roads, carrying heavy traffic, to narrow lanes, where there's only room for single-file traffic. Unless signs show otherwise, the national speed limit will apply but that limit is the maximum speed you may drive – it does not indicate that it's safe to drive at that speed. You must determine the safe speed using your judgement, while taking account of the visibility, signs, hazards and other traffic, as well as road and weather conditions.

You need to be able to deal with

- poor visibility due to bends, hedgerows and steep roadsides
- gradients and camber
- junctions and entrances
- vulnerable road users, including pedestrians, cyclists and horse riders
- slow-moving agricultural machinery
- darkness and various weather conditions.

You need to know

- the MSM and PSL routines
- what the different road signs mean
- the importance of forward planning
- how to scan ahead to anticipate hazards that could be just out of sight
- how to use passing places.

Remember

There are often no pavements on country roads and pedestrians will be walking on the road.

Should I sound the horn if I come across livestock on the road?

Animals will probably be startled by the sound of your horn and their response may be unpredictable. Be patient and pass them slowly.

How fast should I drive?

Always drive so that you can stop within the distance you can see to be clear. Allow more distance when the road is wet or slippery.

Tips from the experts

If you come across mud on the road, it's likely that the vehicle responsible is not far away. Be prepared to find an agricultural vehicle up ahead.

When there are no pavements, pedestrians are advised to walk facing the traffic. This means they'll be on your side of the road. Have this in mind when the road bends and you cannot see what's ahead.

Country roads do not have street lighting. Make sure you use your vehicle's headlights, and switch to dipped headlights so that you do not dazzle oncoming drivers.

Remember

Always drive slowly and quietly past horses and leave them as much room as you can.

Recap question

Q1   What hazards would you expect to find on country roads?

Reflection

Have you ever considered how your driving might be viewed by someone else? If you were in charge of a horse, walking or cycling along the road, how would you like drivers to behave? Is anything stopping you from driving that way?

Accompanying driver advice p152

More information is available here HC r154–156, 214 DES s10

Dual carriageways

Some dual carriageways share the same speed limit as motorways and you join some dual carriageways from a slip road, in a similar way to joining a motorway. Unlike a motorway, though, dual carriageways can have junctions and roundabouts where traffic can join, leave, cross and turn right from the carriageway.

You need to be able to

- drive safely on urban and rural dual carriageways and clearways
- join a dual carriageway – if there's a slip road, use it to adjust your speed to match any vehicles on the dual carriageway and join where there's a suitable gap. If there's no slip road, join as you would on any other road
- choose the correct lane. Before leaving, you should move into the correct lane in good time
- turn right off a dual carriageway.

You need to know

- the MSM and PSL routines (see pages 38 to 39)
- the various speed limits that may be used on dual carriageways
- how to respond to advance warning and information signs
- what you should do if your vehicle breaks down, including the use of your hazard warning lights and warning triangles
- how the weather can affect driving on dual carriageways – for example, when it's wet, how spray from other vehicles may affect visibility.

When can I use the right-hand lane?

On some dual carriageways, the lane on the right may be used for traffic turning right as well as for overtaking. If you're overtaking, watch for clues that traffic ahead of you is slowing down to turn right.

Can you overtake on the left-hand side of another vehicle?

You should not normally overtake on the left, but you can if the traffic is moving slowly in queues and the queue in the right-hand lane is moving more slowly.

Tips from the experts

If there's no slip road, join as you would on any other road. If you're turning right onto a dual carriageway, make sure that the central reservation is deep enough to protect your vehicle. If it is not, you'll have to wait until the carriageway is clear in both directions before you start to cross.

When travelling on a dual carriageway at the national speed limit, remember that situations can change very quickly – use your mirrors frequently so that you always know what's happening around you.

What to expect on your driving test

If possible, your examiner will take you onto a road where the national speed limit applies, and watch to make sure that you join the road safely. Use your mirrors effectively, and take account of the higher speed limit.

Recap questions

Q1   Which lane should you normally drive in when travelling on a dual carriageway?

Q2   If you break down on a dual carriageway, how far away from your vehicle should you place a warning triangle?

Reflection

Have you noticed how some dual carriageways have speed limits below the national speed limit? Why do you think that is? How will it affect your driving along this stretch of road?

Accompanying driver advice p154

More information is available here HC r137–138, 173, 274 DES s8

Motorway driving

Learner drivers can have driving lessons on motorways but only with an approved driving instructor (ADI) and in a car fitted with dual controls that's clearly displaying L plates. However, motorway driving is not part of the practical driving test. The Highway Code has specific rules about motorway driving (r253 to 273), though many of the other rules apply to motorway driving too.

Your ADI will be able to tell you when you're ready to take lessons on the motorway. It's recommended that this only takes place near to the end of your training, when you're ready to take your practical driving test.

You should be competent and in full control of the vehicle. You need to know how to

- join and leave motorways, using acceleration and deceleration lanes
- make effective use of your mirrors
- look and plan further ahead than you would on single carriageways
- respond to other road users
- use the correct lane
- keep a safe separation distance
- respond to signals, road signs and markings
- avoid fatigue, and use service areas
- overtake
- deal with side winds and turbulence
- recognise and use smart motorways with active traffic management (ATM)
- deal with contraflows and roadworks
- deal with accidents and breakdowns
- use the hard shoulder.

Remember

Motorways are the safest of our roads as only 4% of crashes happen on motorways and account for just 5% of all fatalities. When they do occur, however, they tend to be serious because of the speeds involved.

Reflection

Why do you think that some drivers are worried about driving on motorways? Would it help to have some motorway practice with your ADI before you drive alone on a motorway? Why do you think that the most common reason for vehicles breaking down on motorways is running out of fuel?

More information is available here HC r253–273 DES s11

Parking

Whether you're parking at the side of the road or using a bay in a car park, you need to gain the skills to do this safely before you drive on your own.

You need to be able to safely reverse your vehicle into a parked position at the side of the road or in a parking bay. This involves

- co-ordinating your hand and foot controls well, so that your car moves smoothly whether on level ground or on a slope
- keeping a reasonable distance from other vehicles
- observing all around while you're manoeuvring
- using your judgement to perform this manoeuvre accurately, signalling where it's necessary
- having confidence so that you do not take too long to park to avoid becoming a danger or obstruction to other road users.

When parking your vehicle, you need to be aware of

- other road users – keep looking all around and do not just rely on your mirrors
- where you're allowed to park that's legal, safe and convenient.

Starting position The position you start from is important. Pull up parallel with and reasonably close to the vehicle in front of the parking place. Position your car level with or slightly ahead of the parked vehicle.

Intermediate stages You should be able to reverse into the space behind the parked vehicle, within the space of about 2 car lengths. Make sure that you do not hit the kerb while you're doing this.

Finishing position Before you finish manoeuvring, make sure that your car is reasonably close to and parallel with the kerb.

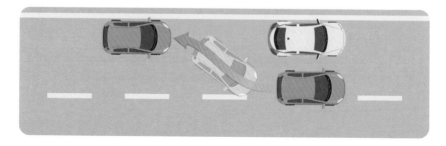

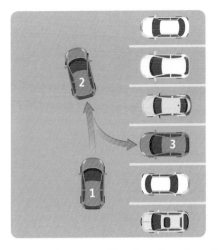
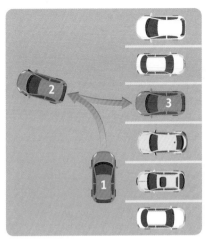

Reverse into a parking bay: 2 options. Follow the steps from 1 to 3.

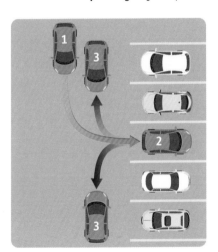
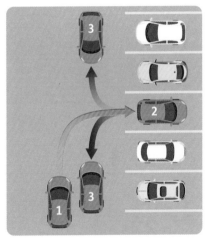

Forward park and reverse out to the left or right: 2 options. Follow the steps from 1 to 3.

Tips from the experts

When parking in a bay, there may be times when the layout would make it easier to turn first so that you can back into the parking space.

What to expect on your driving test

Your examiner will ask you to do one manoeuvre involving reversing. This may be the 'stop on the right-hand side of the road' manoeuvre (see pages 68 to 69) or a reverse parking manoeuvre. If you're asked to reverse park, it could be either

- a parallel park at the side of the road, or
- parking in a bay, either
- driving forwards into a parking bay in a car park and reversing out to the left or right, or
- reversing into a parking bay at the test centre. If you do this at the start of the test, you'll then drive away. If you do it at the end of the test, you will not be asked to drive out again.

Your examiner will tell you which manoeuvre to do, and when.

Recap questions

Q1   Give examples of road markings that indicate you must not park at any time.

Q2   When are you required to leave your parking lights switched on?

Reflection

Do you feel uncomfortable reversing your car into a parking space? Have you ever driven past parking spaces because you could not judge how much room you needed? Why do you think you feel that way and what could you do to improve?

Accompanying driver advice p156

More information is available here HC r202, 238–252 DES s9

Emergency stop

Effective scanning and reading of the road ahead will cut down the risk of having to make an emergency stop. If it's unavoidable, brake as quickly as possible while keeping the car under full control.

You need to know

- how to co-ordinate the brake and clutch pedals so that the car comes to a halt under full control
- the limitations of anti-lock braking systems (ABS)
- how different road and weather conditions can affect the way you stop safely
- how to control a skid if one occurs
- how to move away safely again after you've made an emergency stop.

 Remember

Although you need to know how to stop safely in an emergency, it's important that you know how to avoid having to do so by using your hazard perception skills to plan ahead. You should always drive in such a way that you're aware of situations that might develop and have time to respond to them safely.

Look for this symbol on your dashboard. If the light comes on while you're driving, it means there's a fault with the anti-lock braking system. Any fault with your vehicle's brakes should be checked immediately.

What should I do if my car starts to skid?

If your vehicle does not have ABS, first release the pressure on the brake pedal and then firmly reapply the brakes. If the car skids again, repeat this process. For cars fitted with ABS, see the advice in the owner's manual.

How do I know whether the car I'm driving has ABS?

ABS is fitted to all modern cars. There will be a warning light on the dashboard and advice will be given in the handbook. Also, ask your instructor to demonstrate how ABS works.

Tips from the experts

React quickly, keep both hands on the wheel and try to stop in a straight line without allowing the car to swing off course.

Know the car you're driving – if the car has ABS, make sure you understand how to use the system.

If you have to do this exercise on your driving test, do not try to anticipate the signal that the examiner will give you.

What to expect on your driving test

You may not have to do this exercise on your test but, if you do, your examiner will ask you to pull up at the side of the road. They'll explain the exercise and show you what the signal will be.

Before giving the signal to stop, your examiner will check the road behind to make sure it's safe. When you're given the signal, try to stop the car as you would in a real emergency.

Recap questions

Q1   What happens if the wheels lock?

Q2   In what conditions would ABS brakes not work as effectively as they would normally?

Reflection

Have you ever had to stop in an emergency situation? Did you feel you had the car under control? Was there anything you could have done to prevent the situation becoming an emergency?

Having good tread on your tyres is important. Tyres with worn tread can increase how long it takes to stop in an emergency.

Accompanying driver advice p158

More information is available here HC r117–120 DES s5

Independent driving and using a sat nav

Independent driving is an exercise you'll have to carry out during your driving test. You'll have to follow directions from a sat nav or follow a series of traffic signs. This gives you the chance to experience what it will be like to drive after you've passed your test. You can acquire this key skill while learning, so that you're ready to drive alone.

To drive independently and keep full control, you need to

- plan ahead so that you do not have to make any late decisions
- be able to follow sat nav directions and traffic signs
- use the MSM and PSL routines (pages 38 to 39)
- position your car correctly and in good time
- understand the correct use of lanes, both with and without directional information
- respond correctly to other road users
- know and respond to traffic signs and road markings.

Remember

You will not be prompted when to begin the MSM/PSL routine. Plan well ahead and start the routine in good time.

What will happen if I go off route?

If you take a wrong turning, keep calm. Your examiner will guide you back onto the original route and make sure that you know where you're expected to go.

How will I know where to turn?

Your examiner will supply a sat nav and set the route. You have to follow the directions given by the sat nav. One in 5 driving tests will not use a sat nav; you'll have to follow traffic signs instead.

Tips from the experts

Look and plan well ahead. Give signals in good time but not too early or you may mislead other road users, especially if there's another turning before your junction.

If you realise you're taking the wrong turning, do not make a sudden change of direction, as this could cause a collision. It's better to complete the turn safely and then find somewhere safe to turn around and rejoin your route.

What to expect on your driving test

This part of the test will last around 20 minutes.

Most candidates will be asked to follow directions from a sat nav provided by the examiner.

The examiner will supply the sat nav and set the route, so it does not matter what make or model of sat nav you use while you're practising.

If you're not sure where you're going, you'll be able to ask the examiner to explain again. It will not matter if you go the wrong way unless you make a driving fault.

Recap questions

Q1 How do I know when to start driving independently?

Q2 Will I be told which lane to use?

Reflection

Have you ever made a sudden change of direction because you did not plan ahead? Why did you find yourself in that position? How can you be better prepared in future?

Accompanying driver advice p159

More information is available here HC r170–190 DES s7

Darkness

There are many factors that make driving in the dark more hazardous. Judging speed at night can be difficult, so be particularly careful at junctions.

You need to be confident driving on

- urban roads, where the variety of different lights, such as vehicle lights, street lights and shop signs, can be distracting
- rural roads, where the main source of light will be from vehicle headlights
- single and dual carriageways, where there may be a mixture of lighting.

You should know

- how darkness limits your visibility and therefore your speed, especially in bad weather
- when you need to use your lights, which lights to use and the importance of keeping them clean
- when you can use your horn at night
- how to park safely and legally when it's dark.

Remember

Even within the range of your lights you cannot see as clearly as you would during daylight. Pedestrians, especially those wearing dark clothing, can be difficult to see.

What should I do if I'm following a slow-moving vehicle at night?

Before you overtake you must make sure the road ahead is clear. There may be cyclists, pedestrians or obstructions in the road that are not lit. If you do overtake, do not dazzle the driver of the vehicle in front. Only switch your headlights onto main beam when you've passed the slow-moving vehicle.

What should I do if I'm dazzled by oncoming headlights?

Try not to look directly at the oncoming headlights – slow down and stop if it's necessary. Do not retaliate by leaving your headlights on full beam to dazzle the oncoming driver.

Tips from the experts

You should always drive so that you can stop safely within the distance you can see to be clear. At night, this means within the range of your lights.

Your lights are there to help you to be seen by others as well as to help you see. Make sure that you switch your headlights on as soon as it starts to get dark, and that you do not switch them off until you're sure it's light enough to do so safely.

When following or meeting other vehicles, dip your headlights so that they do not dazzle other drivers.

Judging speed and distance at night can be difficult. Be particularly careful at junctions.

What to expect on your driving test

If conditions require it, your examiner will watch to make sure that you

- use your lights correctly
- drive so that you can stop safely within the distance you can see to be clear.

Recap questions

Q1 At night, when can you park on the side of the road without any lights?

Q2 When may you use your horn at night?

Reflection

Have you ever been dazzled by the headlights of an oncoming vehicle? What did you do? What might happen if you deliberately dazzled the driver of an oncoming vehicle?

Accompanying driver advice p161

More information is available here HC r112–115, 248–252 DES s13

Weather conditions

You need to be aware of the effect some weather conditions, such as fog and low sun, can have on visibility. Other conditions, such as ice, snow and rain, can affect the way that your vehicle handles.

You should be confident in all weather conditions, including

- **fog** – remember, fog is often patchy, so your visibility can change very quickly
- **ice and snow** – check weather forecasts and only travel if it's absolutely necessary
- **bright sunshine** – be aware of the glare this may cause, especially when the road is wet or the sun is low
- **wind** – you may be affected by gusts of wind around buildings, on bridges or other exposed stretches of road
- **rain** – wet roads mean longer stopping distances. Your visibility may also be affected by spray from other vehicles.

You need to know

- the way that different weather conditions affect your visibility, speed and stopping distance. You need to demonstrate that you can respond to these conditions safely
- your vehicle's capabilities and how to use its features; for example, does it have fog lights or four-wheel drive?
- the warning signs and signals that may be used
- the causes of skidding and aquaplaning, and how to control them if they do occur
- when to use your lights and which lights to use in poor daytime visibility.

Remember

When the roads are wet, your stopping distance may be doubled. In icy conditions, you may need to allow 10 times the normal stopping distance.

What if it becomes foggy?

Slow right down; it's much more difficult to judge distances and the speed of other vehicles in fog. Use dipped headlights – and fog lights when visibility is seriously reduced.

What do I do if the road is flooded?

If the water is shallow, drive on slowly. If you are not sure then do not drive into the flood. It might be too deep for your vehicle, the current may be strong, and there may be hidden obstacles under the water. If you do drive through flood water, remember to test your brakes afterwards.

Tips from the experts

Always keep your windscreen, mirrors and windows clean and clear, so that you can see as much as possible all around.

You may not be affected by high winds, but be aware that other road users, such as cyclists, motorcyclists and drivers of high-sided vehicles, are more vulnerable and may be blown into your path.

When visibility is reduced by fog, use dipped headlights and, if the distance you can see falls below 100 metres (328 feet), use your front and rear fog lights. If you do use fog lights, remember to switch them off when visibility improves.

It's not only bad weather that can cause difficult driving conditions. The glare of the sun – especially when the sun is low in the sky in winter – can make it very difficult to see other road users.

What to expect on your driving test

Your examiner will watch to see how you cope with the weather conditions prevailing during the test. You should be capable of operating the windscreen wipers, demisters and lights confidently and without prompting.

Recap questions

Q1 What are the main causes of skidding?

Q2 Why is it dangerous to leave your rear fog lights on if conditions improve?

Reflection

Have you ever been on a journey that was affected by the weather conditions? What weather conditions would make you postpone your journey?

Accompanying driver advice p163

More information is available here HC r226–237 DES s12

Fuel-efficient driving

Everything from the type of car and its fuel consumption to the way in which you drive influences the environment. You need to understand how to minimise the negative effects and how to contribute to keeping the air we breathe cleaner.

You need to understand how driving affects the environment and be aware of

- the effect that vehicle exhaust gases have on the climate, your health, and the health and safety of others
- how you can reduce fuel consumption by changing your driving style
- new technologies offering clean alternatives to fossil fuels.

To minimise your effect on the environment, you need to know how to

- reduce your fuel consumption by planning ahead and using the highest possible gear without making the engine struggle
- make sure your vehicle is serviced as per manufacturer's recommendations and is in a good condition
- check your car's tyre pressures – tyre pressure can have a significant effect on fuel efficiency
- dispose of vehicle waste, such as spent oil, old batteries and used tyres, correctly.

Remember

Many of the suggestions for reducing environmental impact will also reduce your motoring costs.

Does my speed really affect my fuel consumption?

Yes, it makes a big difference. If you travel at 70 mph (112 km/h), you're likely to use up to 15% more fuel than if you covered the same distance at 50 mph (80 km/h).

Does the car I buy make a big difference?

In some cities, low emission zones exist (London has an ultra-low emission zone) where drivers of vehicles that have emissions above set levels have to pay a charge. For further information about fuel and carbon-dioxide emissions, check **www.gov.uk**

Tips from the experts

Use your hazard perception skills to plan ahead, so that you can avoid heavy braking and brisk acceleration. Driving smoothly can reduce your fuel consumption by about 15%, as well as reducing the wear and tear on your vehicle.

Reverse into a parking space so that you can drive out of it. Manoeuvring when the engine is cold uses lots of fuel. Do not over-rev your engine in a low gear.

Check tyre pressures regularly. Incorrect tyre pressure results in a shorter tyre life and may be dangerous. Under-inflated tyres can increase fuel consumption.

Try to avoid using your car for very short journeys, especially when the engine is cold. Consider car sharing or using public transport where you can.

What to expect on your driving test

Your fuel-efficient driving style will be assessed during your driving test. Any faults will be recorded, but they will not affect the result of your test. You'll also be asked questions that test your understanding of environmental issues during your theory test.

Recap question

Q1 What fuels exist that are an alternative to petrol or diesel?

Reflection

What's stopping you changing your driving style to one that's more fuel efficient? Where could you find help to make the change?

Electrically powered vehicles are becoming more available. They produce no direct emissions and can be charged using renewable sources of electricity.

Accompanying driver advice p164

More information is available here HC r123 DES s17

Passengers and loads

As a driver, you need to understand the responsibilities that you have to any passengers, whether they're adults or children, and also how to secure any items that you're transporting.

When carrying passengers and loads, you should be aware of

- your responsibility to other adults, children, babies and animals in your car
- the safest way to carry loads in and on your car
- how to load trailers safely.

You need to know

- the rules concerning the use of seat belts, especially when you're responsible
- the importance of not putting a rear-facing baby seat into a seat that's protected by an airbag
- the importance of checking that all doors are shut properly and that animals are safely restrained
- how to stow luggage or load it securely and the importance of distributing weight evenly.

Remember

Do not overload your car with passengers. Ensure that everyone is wearing a seat belt before you start.

What do I do if a trailer I'm towing starts to weave from side to side?

Try to avoid this happening by distributing the weight properly in the trailer. If it does happen, ease off the accelerator to reduce speed gently.

Can I tow a trailer without taking another test?

You can tow a small trailer under 750 kg maximum authorised mass (MAM) without having to take another test. You may also be able to tow a larger trailer (see page 191).

Tips from the experts

Specially designed roof boxes are streamlined so they'll save fuel as well as carry the load safely.

Special cycle racks fitted on top of or behind the car allow you to carry cycles securely. If they're fitted behind the car, make sure that the number plates and lights can still be seen clearly.

If you're carrying a load, make sure that it's secure and that it does not stick out dangerously.

Heavy loads can have an effect on the handling of your car – changes to the weight and centre of gravity will affect the steering and braking. Allow more stopping distance when you're carrying a heavy load. You may also need to increase your tyre pressures and adjust your headlights (see your vehicle handbook).

What to expect on your driving test

You'll be asked questions about passengers and carrying loads during your theory test.

Recap questions

Q1 Who's responsible for ensuring that children under 14 wear a seat belt?

Q2 What's the speed limit for a car towing a trailer travelling on a single carriageway road?

Reflection

Have you ever thought about the safety of your passengers? How does that make you feel?

Make sure anything you carry is loaded securely and that your vehicle is not overloaded.

Accompanying driver advice p165

More information is available here HC r99–102 DES s2

Security

This covers not only the security of your vehicle but also its contents and your personal security. You need to be aware of the ways that you can reduce the risks.

You need to be aware of your personal safety. You should

- stay alert at all times
- let someone know where you're going and when you expect to arrive or return
- keep important or valuable items locked away from view while they're in your car
- choose a secure place to leave your car, especially at night.

To safeguard your vehicle, you should

- find a secure place to park
- fit additional security measures, such as a steering-wheel lock and immobiliser.

Remember

If possible, park your car in an attended or secure car park. For information and to search for approved sites, visit **parkmark.co.uk**

When should I lock away my valuables?

Criminals could be observing your actions in the car park. Try to lock valuables away before leaving home.

Where can I get advice about vehicle security?

Speak to your local crime prevention officer, who will advise you on devices and any vehicle watch schemes that may operate in your area.

Tips from the experts

An alarm or immobiliser, a visible security device such as a steering-wheel lock or having the registration number etched on all the windows can deter a would-be thief.

Before you leave your car, make sure that you remove all valuables (or at least lock them out of sight), close all the windows and then lock the doors.

If you have to park on the side of the road at night, leave your car in a well-lit area.

Carry a mobile phone so that you can use it to call for help if you break down, are involved in an incident or feel threatened in any way.

Always lock your car even if it's for a short time, such as when paying for petrol.

A steering-wheel lock is a good visible device you can use to improve the security of your vehicle.

What to expect on your driving test

You'll be asked questions about vehicle security during your theory test.

Recap question

Q1 What measures can you take to protect your personal safety when parking at night?

Reflection

Do you ever leave your car unlocked while you pay for fuel? How would you feel if your car was stolen as a result of your actions?

Accompanying driver advice p167

More information is available here HC r239, p131 DES s20

Safe Driving for Life

Driver & Vehicle Standards Agency

Does driving ever make you feel **nervous, angry** or **frustrated**?

Do you want to know how you can **beat stress** and enjoy your driving?

Would you like to **boost your confidence** and **stay up to date** with the latest rules of the road?

The Official DVSA Guide to **Better Driving**
Helping you through a lifetime of safe driving

If the answer to any of these questions is yes, then **Better Driving** is for you.

Book and eBook available, RRP £11.99.

Save 10%*

Order online at **www.safedrivingforlife.info/shop** quoting **SD10** at the checkout, or call **01603 696979** quoting **SD10** to receive **10%** discount.

 @safedrivinglife

safedrivinglife

 safe.driving.for.life

 safedrivingforlifeinfo

TSO (The Stationery Office) is proud to be DVSA's official publishing partner. TSO pays for the marketing of all the products we publish. Images and prices are correct at time of going to press but subject to change without notice. The Stationery Office Limited is registered in England No. 3049649 at 1–5 Poland Street, Soho, London, W1F 8PR. * Apps and eBooks are not included in the promotional discount.

11443 09/19

Section two

💬 Accompanying driver advice

In this section, you'll learn about

- the role of an accompanying driver
- the legal requirements
- setting up your car
- the attitude you'll need
- practising the key skills.

Accompanying a learner

When you accompany a learner driver, you're part of the process of making them a safe driver. Look on it as a team effort involving you, your learner and their ADI.

If you feel unsure about anything or want a bit of advice, you can talk to the ADI about the areas that concern you. You may want to accompany your learner on their next lesson to see how the ADI copes with situations you find difficult. Make sure that your learner is happy for you to sit in and arrange a suitable time with their ADI.

Sometimes the ADI may teach a driving technique that seems wrong to you. Remember, as cars become more sophisticated, so recommended techniques change to take advantage of new technology.

The ADI is probably using the most up-to-date methods, which may be different from the way you were taught. Do not confuse your learner by expecting them to do things 'your way'. One part of your role is to enable your learner to practise the techniques taught by their ADI.

Can you do it legally?

Before you agree to accompany a learner driver, there are a few things you need to check.

1   Have you held a full EC/EEA driving licence for at least 3 years for the category of vehicle being driven?
2   Are you at least 21 years of age?
3   Is the car you intend to use insured for use by the learner?
4   Is the car fitted with L plates (D plates in Wales) to both the front and rear of the car?
5   Is the car you intend to use in a safe, roadworthy condition?

The answer must be YES to all questions before you can act as an accompanying driver to a learner.

Remember

Working together is the best way of helping your learner towards a lifetime of safe driving.

Getting started

Beginning

For a new driver, there's an awful lot to learn. This includes

- a good knowledge of driving theory
- learning how to operate a complicated set of controls (which looks so easy)
- operating the controls while putting the theory into practice
- developing good judgement
- anticipation and awareness.

As well as developing these skills, the new driver needs to learn to cope with

- other road users
- the weather
- road conditions
- navigation.

Remember

New drivers cannot begin driving until they've received their licence from the Driver and Vehicle Licensing Agency (DVLA) and it has come into effect.

Even after basic control skills have developed, being able to cope with constantly changing demands and unexpected events – often in a fraction of a second – is a skill that comes with experience.

It's complicated, challenging and, for some, extremely difficult. To expect that all this can be learned in a few short lessons is a mistake.

A learner driver needs to gain enough skill and experience to enable them to drive alone safely once they've passed their driving test. As more miles are driven and more experience is gained, the novice driver will gradually progress towards becoming an experienced driver.

Driving is a subject where there are always new lessons to be learned and it's a foolish and dangerous driver who thinks they know it all.

So how does a learner begin the process of going from novice to competent safe driver? The answer lies in 2 key areas

Training – to learn new skills

Practice – to gain experience.

Training

Most people learn to drive with an ADI. Driving instructors are professionals who are trained to teach driving skills in a structured manner to suit differing abilities.

Remember

Some insurance companies do not insure people under 25 years of age, while others may offer reduced premiums for new drivers who complete the Pass Plus scheme (see pages 187 to 188).

Do not risk driving uninsured!

Many pupils only have one or two hours of professional driving instruction each week and their experience is often limited to driving at the same time of day and over the same types of road.

Where you fit in

As an accompanying driver, you'll be helping your learner have more practice and gain wider experience of the varied driving conditions they're likely to meet once they've passed their driving test.

Once you're ready to take on this responsibility, you need to think about developing the skills of your learner – know their limits and do not attempt any driving that will be beyond their ability.

Remember

Learners who combine extra practice with professional lessons not only perform better on their driving test but go on to have a reduced incident rate in the early years of driving unaccompanied.

You're helping a new driver to gain skills that will help to keep them safe for many years to come.

That's not to say it will be an easy task. There may be times when you need to remind yourself why you're there.

 Remember

Do not forget that only an ADI can charge for driving lessons. Even accepting money for fuel is an offence unless you're an ADI. Do not be caught out.

What can you expect?

To start with, do not expect this to be easy. Learning to drive takes a lot longer than most people realise. You need to set aside plenty of time for practice sessions in order for your learner to develop their skills properly.

If you set dates and times when you're expecting to go out with your learner, you're more likely to be in a calm frame of mind than if you've had to stop what you were doing and grudgingly give your time.

Be guided by the ADI, but once the basic skills have been learned, it's a good idea to let your learner do a lot of the everyday driving, such as to the shops or to school or college.

If your learner struggles with something you think is easy, do not worry. Everyone learns at different rates and in different ways, and it may be necessary to go over the same ground many times.

The memory often plays tricks and you may have forgotten how you struggled with some aspects of learning to drive.

 Remember

Young drivers are about twice as likely as older drivers to be involved in a road traffic incident when negotiating a bend.

What are you expecting to achieve?

By helping a learner driver to practise, you're helping them to develop

- confidence and competence using their new skills
- a sound basis on which to build their driving career
- enough experience to be able to think for themselves and cope safely with any driving situation they meet
- confidence about their ability to pass the driving test
- an understanding of their responsibility as a driver.

The practice vehicle

Is your car suitable for your learner to drive? A learner may learn in any make or model of car, but a large, powerful car may be more difficult to control than a smaller model.

Small cars are not necessarily any easier to drive but their size can make judging the car's position easier, especially during manoeuvres.

It might be helpful to find a driving school that uses a similar car to your own. If this is not possible, make allowances for your learner if they struggle to adapt to your car after lessons in the school car.

> **Remember**
>
> Fit an extra rear-view mirror. Knowing what's going on behind is important for safety and peace of mind.

L plates – Avoid fixing L (D) plates to the windscreen or rear window, since they restrict the view. Do not forget to cover or remove the L (D) plates when the car is being used by a full licence-holder.

Make sure the L (or D) plates are secure. You do not want them to fly off at higher speeds.

Attitude

Bad habits

It's too easy for bad habits to creep unnoticed into anyone's driving. Before you act as an accompanying driver, it's worth looking at your own driving. You'll have little credibility if you expect your learner to drive one way while you practise another – and do not expect your learner not to notice. Why not have a lesson or two with the ADI yourself? This will allow an expert to check your driving and help you to improve your skills.

Drinking and driving, speed limits, use of signals, seat belts and attitude to other road users are all aspects of driving where standards might slip. Setting a good example when you drive will have positive benefits for both you and your learner.

Patience

Frustration can soon set in when your learner struggles with something you think should be easy, or they cannot do something that they could do the last time you went out. If something is proving difficult, do not keep trying it until tempers fray. Leave it and come back to it another time. Learning to drive should be an enjoyable experience, not an ordeal.

Other road users may be inconsiderate and show little regard for the fact that your driver is a learner. Do not allow this to annoy you, since it will also affect your learner. Knocking a learner driver's confidence can ruin their driving career before it has even started.

Technique

Before accompanying your learner, you should give some thought to how you're going to

- give directions
- cope with dangerous situations.

Remember

Learning to drive takes a lot longer than most people think.

Be patient with your learner.

Your learner will need clear directions, given calmly and in plenty of time. You'll need to look and think that bit further ahead than normal. If your learner has difficulty telling their right from their left, you'll need to overcome this problem. Your ADI should be able to give you some advice on these matters, as well as tips on giving directions at any complex junctions in your area.

Safety is your priority. Where possible, you should act early to prevent hazards from developing into dangerous situations. If a dangerous situation does develop, you may need to

- speak firmly and clearly without shouting
- reach across and take control of the steering
- use the parking brake
- use dual controls if your car has them fitted.

Avoiding conflicts

Accompanying a novice driver can be frustrating, unnerving and a lot harder than you think. Here are a few points worth remembering to help you keep on top of it.

- Talking to the ADI will help you plan practice sessions which avoid areas that are too difficult for your learner's present level of ability.
- Learn from mistakes and do not dwell on them. Encouragement and tolerance will help skills and confidence develop.
- Nothing is achieved if you allow yourself to become angry with your learner. If it's all going wrong, have a break for 5 minutes or stop the session altogether if things are too bad.
- If something happens which scares either of you, pull over and give yourselves time to calm down. Discuss what went wrong and why. Were you expecting too much from your learner?
- If another road user fails to show your learner due consideration, do not allow it to upset you. Set a good example, keep calm and turn the experience into a lesson in anticipation.

Remember

Keep reminding yourself that you're making a big difference to your learner's long-term driving safety. Learners rarely have crashes while practising.

- Prevent your learner from getting into difficulties by looking well ahead so you can anticipate problems. Do not expect them to have the same degree of awareness and judgement as you.

- Your learner is going to drive in the way their instructor has taught. If any techniques differ from the way you drive, do not argue over who's right or insist they do it your way. Make a note and discuss it with the ADI.

Planning

When to start

DVSA recommends that new drivers reach a level of proficiency with an ADI before starting to practise with an accompanying driver. Ask the ADI to tell you when your learner is ready to start practising. Starting too soon may be unnerving for both of you and could lead to anything from a loss of confidence through to a serious loss of control.

Remember

A learner driver may find driving very tiring. Many crashes involving young drivers result from lack of experience.

Use the 'Driver's Record' to see the progress being made and the topics needing practice. To start with, this will mostly be control skills, but it will gradually move on to include the whole syllabus.

Early days

Before you begin your first practice sessions, you need to give some thought to where and when you're going to conduct them. When you begin, driving in heavy traffic at rush hour is not going to be good for either of you.

Where Pick a quiet area where

- there will not be much traffic to deal with
- you will not cause a nuisance to other road users or local residents.

It's also a good idea to find somewhere fairly level because of the added difficulties a hill can create at this stage.

Your learner will probably drive quite slowly and, despite your efforts to find somewhere quiet, you may find a queue of traffic building up behind. If this happens, be prepared to ask your learner to pull over somewhere safe and let the traffic pass.

When Plan the first few practice sessions to avoid busy times of the day. These include peak commuting hours, school start and finish times, and during local events.

Your learner can only practise when you make the time available. Work and other commitments may make demands on you and the only time you have could be evenings and weekends.

In the winter months, evening practice will be in the dark – but do not let this be an excuse not to practise. As long as the weather conditions are not dangerous, practising in the dark should not be a problem.

During Remember that you're in charge of the vehicle even when the learner is driving. You need all your concentration for supervising the learner – you **MUST NOT** use your mobile phone or other hand-held device at any time while the provisional licence-holder is driving a motor vehicle on a road (see page 22).

Planning your sessions

Many learners take their driving lessons at the same time of day and drive repeatedly on the same types of road.

While this may provide a level of familiarity with these roads, it does little to provide a broad experience of the wide variety of driving conditions your learner will meet when they've passed their test.

 Remember

Could your learner cope with any situation that might arise? They'll have to when they pass their test.

Good practice sessions should build both experience and confidence. This can be achieved by planning each session around your learner's requirements and their driving limitations. Check their 'Driver's Record' to see which topics need practising.

As part of your planning, you'll need to think about routes, time of day, road types, manoeuvring and weather conditions. These are now looked at in turn.

Routes Thinking through where you're going to take your learner will enable you to

- avoid areas that may have features, such as a steep hill or a difficult junction, which they're not yet ready for
- practise certain aspects, such as left turns, traffic lights, one-way streets.

You do not want to put your learner into a situation that they cannot cope with and could have been avoided if you'd planned ahead.

Time of day Local knowledge will tell you which roads are busiest and when. This will allow you to avoid the worst areas in the early days, and practise in heavy traffic when your learner is ready.

Daylight, dusk and darkness are driving conditions that require different skills, which need to be practised. If your learner has great difficulty seeing at night, have their night vision tested by an optician.

Your learner should be able to think independently and use the car's lights correctly and when necessary.

Road types Unless you're an ADI, you cannot accompany a learner driver on the motorway (see pages 21, 76 to 77). You can help them to practise on all other types of road. If a 'Driver's Record' is being used, it will indicate the types of road where practice is needed.

Manoeuvring The driving test requires manoeuvres that reflect real driving situations to be demonstrated. These include

- stopping in an emergency
- driving independently by following directions from a sat nav or road signs
- pulling up and reversing on the right-hand side of the road
- parking using reverse gear, both on the road and into/out of car park bays.

The ADI will teach the techniques and, if a 'Driver's Record' is being used, will record which have been taught and which need practice.

Weather conditions Many learners begin learning in the spring months and pass their driving test before winter arrives.

These learners may have had little or no experience of driving in

- rain and slippery conditions
- mist and fog
- windy conditions.

These are everyday conditions that most motorists encounter in their first year of driving. When the ADI indicates your learner is ready to cope with them, be prepared to go out in these conditions as they occur.

Remember

Do not underestimate the weather. Extreme weather can make driving unsafe. It's recommended that you avoid practising in these conditions in the early days.

If in doubt – do not venture out.

Key skills

The following pages (118 to 167) give advice and tips on helping your learner to practise the key skills explained in section 1.

Legal responsibilities

See page 27

Your learner should have a full understanding of their legal responsibilities as a driver. These include

- driving licences and accompanying learner drivers
- vehicle tax (SORN), insurance and MOT
- fitness to drive and driver's eyesight requirements
- New Drivers Act
- dealing with tiredness and fatigue
- traffic rules and regulations
- alcohol and drugs
- mobile phones
- roadworthiness of their vehicle
- dealing with road traffic incidents.

Remember

Ignorance is no excuse in the eyes of the law. Make sure that both your and your learner's knowledge is up to date.

How you can help

Ask questions so that your learner has to think about their responsibilities. If you're both unclear about an issue, then work together to find out the facts. For example, if you did not know about the New Drivers Act, you could ask your ADI to explain it to both of you.

To keep up to date with changes in the law, own and refer to the latest edition of The Highway Code. This is available as a traditional paper book and also as an app on your phone, eBook and online, and can be obtained from **safedrivingforlife.info/shop**.

What to expect

Many new drivers will have an understanding of the issues that directly affect them, such as applying for a driving licence. They may not know about recent changes in the law or matters that you routinely deal with, such as taxing your car.

If you involve your learner, they may not only learn the processes but they may also appreciate the costs associated with owning and running a car.

Safety checks

See page 30

As part of their driving test, your learner will be asked to show and explain basic safety checks necessary to keep their car safe on the road.

The ADI will cover the driving-test requirements but learning how to carry out routine safety checks is not something to learn for the test and then forget. Aspects such as tyre condition are the driver's responsibility. If the tyres are illegal, the driver could be fined or have penalty points added to their driving licence.

How you can help

Before each practice drive, watch while your learner carries out safety checks on the vehicle. Developing a habit of regular checks can also help identify faults at an early stage and this may prevent the vehicle from breaking down during a journey.

Allowing your learner to clean the windscreen, windows, mirrors and lights will help you and will also help them to remember these aspects.

What to expect

Many new drivers do not have an interest in the workings of the car but they do need to understand

- daily and weekly vehicle checks
- service intervals
- MOT requirements.

The importance of having your vehicle regularly serviced should be stressed. You could show your learner how you keep a record of your car's service intervals.

Remember, 'FLOWER'

F Fuel

L Lights and indicators

O Oil (engine, steering and brake fluid)

W Water (engine coolant, windscreen washers)

E Electrics (battery, charging system)

R Rubber (tyres and brakes).

Cockpit checks

See page 33

Your learner will be competent in this topic when they independently

- make a point of checking their door is closed properly
- check and, if necessary, adjust their driving position. This includes adjusting the seat, steering wheel and head restraint
- correctly fasten their seat belt
- check and adjust the mirrors
- check the parking brake is on and the gear lever is in neutral.

Modern cars have both a seat belt warning lamp and a warning beeper. If you drive off without fastening your seat belt, you'll see the warning lamp and the beeper will sound. The light and beeper will continue until you fasten your seat belt.

How you can help

Watch to see that your learner completes their checks before starting the engine. Look to see that each item is checked and not just mentioned.

What to expect

It's not uncommon for learners to find that, once they're on the road, one or more mirrors require some further adjustment, or the seat needs repositioning.

Do not let them try to make adjustments while on the move. Find a safe place for them to pull over and stop before making any further adjustment.

Remember

Mirrors need to be adjusted so that they can be used with the least possible head movement.

Controls and instruments

See page 36

Reading and understanding instruments, such as the speedometer and the fuel and temperature gauges, are essential.

By the time your learner is ready for their test, they should also understand the warning lights and, importantly, know what action to take if one comes on while they're driving.

In the early days of learning to drive, controlling the steering, gears and foot controls will take all your learner's concentration. As their skill develops, it's also important for them to become competent with ancillary controls such as the demister, wipers, heaters and so on.

Remember

Your learner should be able to operate all the controls without looking down to find them.

How you can help

Allow your learner to familiarise themselves with the layout of the controls and instruments, and explain any special features that may be fitted to your car.

The controls may be laid out differently in the ADI's car and this could lead to some confusion; for example, if the windscreen wiper controls are on the left of the steering column instead of on the right.

What to expect

When you're in situations that call for the use of certain controls, such as the front or rear screen demister, your learner may be concentrating really hard on their driving and fail to realise the need to use them.

Do not allow the situation to become dangerous, but do encourage your learner to recognise for themselves when these controls should be used.

If your learner fumbles while trying to find and operate the control they want, pull up somewhere safe and run through the control layout again.

Moving away and stopping

See page 38

Choosing a safe place to stop and stopping safely are things that every driver needs to do. Your learner will also need to develop sound judgement and awareness of other road users.

How you can help

While your learner is having to concentrate really hard on using the controls, they may forget to watch for other road users. Stay alert and do not let them move off into danger. Practise moving off

- on level ground
- uphill
- downhill
- from behind a parked vehicle.

Asking your learner to pick somewhere safe to stop will allow them to think for themselves. They need to look for somewhere to stop and then use their mirrors and signals correctly while bringing the car to rest at their chosen place. When teaching someone to stop, you should advise that a gear change is not always necessary.

What to expect

Every time your learner moves off, expect them to go through a lengthy process of finding the biting point and balancing the accelerator and clutch against the parking brake. This will make moving off a slow process and this, in turn, makes dealing with road junctions more difficult.

Frustration may set in as

- traffic builds up behind
- your learner cannot pull out into a space that you think is safe.

If you find your learner has difficulty with busy junctions, avoid them and pick quieter alternatives until the necessary control skills have developed.

When stopping, watch that your learner does not try to stop suddenly without allowing time for using the mirror and signalling if necessary. Use the extra rear-view mirror to check the traffic behind you.

Remember

Traffic lights are one place where tension can build. When the red light changes, it's not uncommon for novices to stall in their rush to move off promptly. This can lead to panic, especially if there's a queue of traffic behind. Stay calm and do not react to another driver sounding their horn – they may not be able to see the L plates if they are not immediately behind.

Safe positioning

See page 41

With experience, judging the car's position becomes second nature, but learning to position accurately is a surprisingly difficult skill to learn.

Some learners look just in front of the car, rather than well ahead. This makes it more difficult to judge the car's width and position on the road. As well as the control skills, your learner will need to know

- where to position the car for any particular driving situation
- the meaning of signs and road markings.

How you can help

The skill of being able to judge the car's position on the road from the passenger seat will develop with practice. You may need to reach across and steer into the correct position. Try to remain calm and do not allow the wrong road position to go uncorrected for any length of time.

At first, avoid using places such as narrow streets or roads with width restrictions until your learner has developed a little in both confidence and skill. Then you can move them onto areas and roads requiring more accurate judgement.

What to expect

Before your learner's judgement has developed, they may

- drive too close to the kerb, the edge or centre of the road, parked cars, or other obstructions
- position the vehicle poorly around bends and junctions
- show poor lane discipline.

Do not allow your learner to hit the kerb while driving normally. The impact may wrench the steering wheel from their grasp, causing serious loss of control. It may also damage or burst the tyre.

Some mistakes can be scary for you as a passenger but your learner may be unaware of this, or that they've made an error. If it's going wrong, pull over and talk about it. You may need to demonstrate their mistake in order for the learner to realise it for themselves. If you disagree on some aspect of positioning, then discuss it with the ADI.

Correct position is vital when there's not much room, such as narrow roads or lanes.

Mirrors – vision and use

See page 44

The ADI will cover this subject early in the learning process but watch for your learner having to make exaggerated head movements to use the mirrors. This may mean adjustments are needed, once you've stopped in a safe place.

Correctly adjusted mirrors give a good view behind and to the sides of the car. It's important that your learner uses the mirrors when necessary and is aware of the areas not covered by the mirrors (and that they know how and when to check them).

How you can help

When accompanying your learner, look to see if they're checking the mirrors correctly. If a mirror check is missed, you should always draw their attention to it, but avoid prompting them too early – they may become reliant on your prompt rather than thinking for themselves.

Do not let them change direction without first checking that it's safe.

To check if your learner is using their mirrors, fit another small interior mirror on the left of the windscreen, angled so that you can see your learner without having to look directly at them.

Remember

When turning right in busy traffic, there will be occasions when a blind-area check to the right needs to be made in case a vehicle is attempting to overtake. There may be so much else going on that this check is missed and you may need to look for them.

What to expect

When watching your learner's use of mirrors, check

- how well they time their mirror checks
- that they act correctly on what can be seen.

You may find yourself having to look and plan further ahead than normal, so that you can identify hazards early enough to then be watching to see how your learner deals with them. This can have an extra benefit in that it improves your own hazard awareness.

Signals

See page 47

Drivers need to know how and when to give signals and the meaning of signals given by others. Whichever way signals are given, they must be given clearly and in good time. Your learner must be able to identify the signals of others and act correctly on them.

How you can help

Watch your learner's use of signals and make sure they use only signals shown in The Highway Code. Try to use routes that will expose your learner to the need to think about the timing of a signal or whether a signal is appropriate; for example

- when passing a parked car with a road junction on the right
- turning right or left when there's another junction just before your turn.

If in any doubt about the correct procedure, ask the ADI for advice.

If you want to stop on the left just after the junction, it's important you time your signal correctly to avoid misleading the driver waiting at the junction.

What to expect

In the early part of their training, learners will be thinking about their use of the car controls and may forget to signal. This may be dangerous; for example, when pulling up while being followed by another vehicle.

Stay alert and give help in good time if there's a risk to safety. There may be occasions when another road user gives a signal that your learner has not met before, such as reversing lights on a car that's trying to reverse park into a space on the side of the road.

Learners tend to shy away from using the horn. However, it's a valuable aid to road safety when used correctly and you should encourage its use when appropriate.

Most indicators will automatically cancel after a manoeuvre, but sometimes they might not. Do not let an uncancelled signal continue for any length of time – it could mislead another road user and lead to danger.

Remember

The horn must only be used while the vehicle is moving, to make other road users aware of your presence. Refer your learner to The Highway Code, r112.

Anticipation and planning

See page 50

Before your learner can react to a risk, they must perceive that a risk exists. That perception is governed by

- training (in this situation, do this)
- experience (I've met this before and need to do this)
- planning (what should I do now to prevent risk in the situation I can see?)
- anticipation (what if?).

One of the main problems for inexperienced drivers is that they do not recognise the hazard until it's too late to avoid the danger.

How you can help

Practice is so important. During practice, your learner will meet situations that they've never met before. While you're sitting next to them, your experience in both seeing and reacting to any risk should keep them safe and, where possible, you can pass on the benefit of your experience.

While your learner can never experience every type of hazard, you can aim to instil in them a heightened awareness of hazards and a knowledge of how to cope with them.

What to expect

Your learner may feel they have everything under control, but if the way they deal with hazards makes you feel uncomfortable, something is wrong with their driving. When a mistake has been made, you'll need to highlight the potential danger in their response to a situation.

Learners can be defensive about their driving ability and you should take account of their feelings. Stay calm and do not raise your voice, but do make sure they understand the consequences of their actions.

 Remember

New drivers often do not look very far ahead. They can be too slow to identify potential danger and do not realise how soon they need to react. Step in to help before danger develops.

Use of speed

See page 53

Driving too fast is one of the main causes of road traffic incidents on all types of road. Driving too slowly is a different mistake and one that creates its own set of hazards.

So how fast should your learner be driving? What's a suitable speed? The answer is dependent on a number of variables and getting it right takes practice.

Your learner must never drive so fast that there's a risk of them losing control. They must not exceed the speed limit, but they should be able to drive on all roads without hindering the flow of traffic.

How you can help

The more experience your learner has of various driving situations, the better they'll become at assessing the correct speed for different conditions and reacting to changes in the speed limit.

If your learner is timid, remember that it may take a long time before they feel confident in this skill.

If you think your learner is not improving very quickly, do not be negative or critical – a timid driver needs encouragement, not criticism. Learning to drive is a lengthy process, so you'll need to allow more time for practice.

Do not ignore rural roads where wide variations in speed can be experienced, as this will be good practice for your learner. In these rural areas, they'll have to

- plan ahead
- continually adjust their speed.

Remember

Make sure that your learner obeys speed limits and understands that the limit is not a target – it's the maximum speed that's legally permitted.

It is not always safe to drive at the speed limit.

What to expect

You can expect your learner to start by driving slowly in all situations. In particular, expect very slow acceleration up through the gears, which can make emerging at junctions difficult and, for you, frustrating.

For the first few practice sessions, do not let your learner drive the car if you're in a hurry to get somewhere, as this may make you feel impatient.

If you become critical and negative, what sort of message do you think this gives your learner about correct driver behaviour towards other road users?

You need to be patient, tolerant and understanding. As experience and confidence grow, speeds will increase and skills in hazard awareness and planning ahead will develop. However, overconfidence and an irresponsible attitude towards risk need to be discouraged.

The ADI will teach learners how to keep a safe distance from the vehicle in front, but the learner must then put this theory into practice when they drive. Help them practise applying the 2-second rule appropriately and safely until it becomes a habit.

It's vital that your learner understands that they're responsible for the consequences of their driving behaviour.

Other traffic

See page 56

Your learner needs to gain experience in dealing with traffic while having the safety net of an experienced driver sitting by their side. While you cannot cover every possible situation, you should be able to help them learn to deal safely with

- oncoming traffic
- turning across the path of other vehicles
- overtaking
- parked vehicles or other obstructions.

How you can help

These traffic situations call for judgement and often there's little or no room for error. Do not allow your learner to overestimate their own ability or their car's performance. If they make a mistake, you're there to prevent it from developing into something more serious.

Avoid busy main roads until confidence has developed. Try and find places to practise that include

- narrow roads
- parked cars and other obstructions
- roads with right-turn lane markings
- traffic lights
- box junctions.

As well as practising dealing with obstructions on your side of the road, find places where your learner has to anticipate the actions of an approaching driver who might not give way. For hazards that you do not encounter, you can always talk to your learner about possible situations. Thinking about potential danger is a big part of developing hazard awareness.

Remember

You're responsible for ensuring that your learner does not create dangerous situations through inexperience or poor judgement.

What to expect

Learners will usually be cautious; on busy roads, you may wait for some time. Do not become frustrated if you feel that some opportunities are being missed – as confidence builds, so will ability.

When waiting to turn right, you may find oncoming drivers will give way and invite your learner to turn. Before accepting, your learner must check for other road users, such as motorcyclists and cyclists.

When overtaking, many mistakes can be made through inexperience and lack of judgement.

Errors can include

- overtaking too slowly
- overtaking when the vehicle in front is driving close to the speed limit
- not allowing enough room
- cutting in too soon after overtaking.

Also remember that, if your car is different from the ADI's, your learner may take time to get used to judging its width.

When meeting oncoming traffic, your learner needs to judge the available space and, if necessary, give way.

Junctions

See page 59

Dealing with junctions includes driving straight ahead as well as turning right and left. Junctions can be any shape or size, including those with

- road markings
- no road markings
- traffic lights
- warning signs.

Your learner will have to learn where and when they should be looking and what they're looking for. Interpreting what they see and planning how to deal with the possible outcomes is a skill that develops with experience.

Your learner should already be familiar with the signs and markings in The Highway Code, but they first have to see the sign or marking and realise how it affects them before they can act on the information given.

Remember

Do not be fooled by your learner's apparent confidence – their hazard perception skills will not be well developed, even though they think they're observing well and feel everything is under control.

Crossroads call for sound judgement as there may be oncoming vehicles turning as well as passing traffic on the main road.

How you can help

Check the 'Driver's Record' to see which level your learner has reached and plan their practice accordingly.

Try to find junctions where you can practise turning into as well as out of side roads, or one where your learner can drive round a circuit or block.

When planning a location, consider whether

- there will be much traffic
- both turns and emerges can be practised
- there are road markings to help with positioning
- there are any difficulties; for example, steep slopes or poor visibility at any of the junctions.

What to expect

The ADI will already have covered the Mirrors – Signal – Manoeuvre routine for dealing with junctions. However, new learners may be struggling with steering or changing gear while thinking about speed, mirrors, road position and signs.

Remember

If your learner is not confident in their ability to move off, they may try to emerge from a junction without stopping to see if it's safe. If you cannot see that it's safe, neither can they.

Do not let them cause an incident.

In addition, new drivers often do not look very far ahead and may not see, or may misjudge, any approaching traffic. They can also be slow to identify potential danger.

Mistakes can easily happen and a mistake at a junction can be dangerous as well as frightening for both of you. If you cannot see that it's safe, then neither can your learner. Keep calm and step in to help before any danger develops.

Roundabouts

See page 62

Many learners find it difficult to cope with roundabouts. The ADI may ask for them to be practised in stages; for example, turning left, turning right and going ahead. If that's the case, you'll need to plan routes accordingly.

Try to include a variety, from large multi-lane roundabouts to small and mini-roundabouts.

Remember

Rear-end collisions are very common at roundabouts. They're often caused when a driver waiting to join the roundabout does not do so but the driver behind expects them to and moves forward while looking for traffic on the roundabout. Be aware of this hazard at busy roundabouts.

How you can help

When you're approaching a roundabout, tell your learner in plenty of time which direction you want them to go. If possible, use other instructions to help them, such as 'follow the sign to the town centre' or 'the third exit'.

If your learner becomes disorientated, tell them in good time where their exit is, to allow them time to position correctly.

If they miss the exit, do not worry. Direct them round again, using the appropriate lane or road position and take the exit required. You need to encourage your learner to plan their route onto, around and off the roundabout. Try to avoid a situation where your learner is part-way around the roundabout before they start to think about which road they should be taking.

What to expect

If your learner is uncertain of the direction in which they're supposed to be going, expect incorrect signalling and positioning. They may also

- drive too slowly, which can cause problems if there's fast-moving traffic
- veer suddenly to take an exit at the last moment, with no thought for other traffic.

Learners often struggle with directions on roundabouts. Try to get them to make use of the signs, so that they know what to expect.

Pedestrian crossings

See page 64

There are laws governing pedestrian crossings that your learner must know and obey. There are also several types of pedestrian crossing – do you know them all?

How you can help

When your learner is approaching a crossing, see if they can tell you which type of crossing it is and which rules apply.

Going out for a drive at school start and finish times should ensure plenty of opportunities to deal with busy crossings.

Darkness adds another aspect to safely dealing with pedestrian crossings, so practice during twilight or the hours of darkness is also recommended.

What to expect

Noticing there's a crossing ahead is the first hurdle. You'll soon tell if your learner has not spotted it, and you may need to act promptly. However, do not let your learner over-react and stop unnecessarily. This could cause a danger to traffic behind you.

Make certain that they understand the sequence of lights at light-controlled crossings, and react correctly to each phase of the lights.

Remember

Pedestrians are among the most vulnerable road users. If you have any doubts about your learner's ability to cope, give assistance until you're happy that they can cope unaided and without any risk of losing control.

Reversing

See page 67

For many learners, reversing accurately is the most difficult part of learning to drive. If your learner finds reversing difficult, you can expect to spend a lot of time practising this skill.

How you can help

It's easier to begin by practising reversing on the left-hand side of the road before practising on the right-hand side. As skill develops you can move on to manoeuvring, such as reversing into side roads or driveways and parking. The techniques for reversing are described in 'The Official DVSA Guide to Driving – the essential skills'.

Look for a place to practise where

- there's good visibility
- the road is level
- you do not expect much traffic
- you will not annoy local residents.

A crossroads or staggered junction is not a suitable location to practise reversing. Do not just use one location but try to find a variety of places for practice sessions.

What to expect

Reversing does not come easily to many learners. If your learner becomes despondent, move on to another topic and return to reversing practice another day.

Practising on an uphill slope before skills have developed is likely to cause wear on the clutch and noise as the engine is excessively revved. Try to avoid this until your learner has developed some skill and confidence in reversing on flat ground.

Remember

Good all-round observation is essential when reversing.

Modern cars have exterior mirrors fitted on both sides of the car. If these mirrors are used for reversing, remember that

- there's no view directly behind the car
- the driver may focus solely on the detail seen in the mirror and fail to see other road users or obstructions
- the mirrors are not set for rear observation when driving. There are still blind spots that need to be checked by looking around.

Turning the vehicle around

See page 70

The skills required to turn the car around in the road will be needed every time your learner has to manoeuvre in a confined space.

How you can help

You may wish to familiarise yourself with the technique taught by the ADI. This is explained in detail in 'The Official DVSA Guide to Driving – the essential skills'. When looking for a place to practise the exercise, consider

- road width
- visibility
- traffic volume
- local residents.

Be courteous to other road users while your learner is practising. Be prepared to find somewhere else if the first place turns out to be less suitable than you first thought.

What to expect

Some learners can take time to recall techniques they've been taught – panic may set in and disorientation may follow halfway through an exercise. They might struggle with the controls, fail to notice other road users or be unable to judge the car's length. Be supportive and offer encouragement, rather than criticism, if it's all taking longer than you anticipated.

You may temporarily release your seat belt while your pupil is carrying out a manoeuvre that involves the reverse gear, to give a little more freedom in which to teach the exercise safely. However, you **MUST** refasten it once the manoeuvre has been completed.

Remember

A sudden loss of control when turning can cause the vehicle to surge forwards or backwards onto the pavement and collide with whatever is in the way. You'll need to act promptly if your learner loses control in this manner.

Country roads

See page 72

Taking your learner out on country roads is important, especially if most of their driving lessons take place on urban roads. Controlling speed, forward planning and hazard awareness skills are all called for and need plenty of practice.

This might seem easy to an experienced driver, but novice drivers often find it hard and overestimate their ability and underestimate the dangers.

How you can help

When you take your learner out on country roads, try and gauge how far ahead they're thinking. At first it will not be far enough but, over time, they should start to read the signs, and be questioning what might be just out of sight.

There may be speed limit changes as you pass through towns or villages. Try to get your learner to notice the speed limit signs well ahead. Noticing potential hazards early like this means your learner can respond smoothly. Easing off the accelerator to slow down before passing a lower speed limit sign means they will not have to brake as hard, if at all. This saves fuel, reduces wear on brake pads, and gives other road users more time to notice and react as well.

What to expect

In the early stages, your learner might try and drive too fast as they will not appreciate the possible hazards that may lie ahead. Control their speed to make sure that they do not come across a situation they cannot manage.

You may then find that other drivers follow close behind, as they wish to come past but cannot see if it's clear ahead. Do not let this unsettle your learner. If necessary, you could look for a place for them to pull over so that the faster driver can pass.

As your learner's skill improves, they'll be able to drive more quickly. Make sure they keep up their forward planning and, when following another vehicle, that they keep a safe distance behind. Their ADI will have taught them the 2-second rule – make sure they use it.

> **Remember**
>
> More people die each year while driving on country roads than any other type of road. Helping your learner to drive safely is time well spent.

Dual carriageways

See page 74

Dual carriageways are not governed by the same regulations that apply to motorways.

However, driving at higher speeds and in lanes on a dual carriageway is valuable experience both in itself and in preparation for motorway driving.

How you can help

As well as driving in the correct lane on the dual carriageway, your learner needs to gain experience of

- using slip roads
- turning right
- overtaking
- high-speed traffic.

Gaining such experience during adverse weather conditions, in twilight and during the hours of darkness is also very valuable.

What to expect

Most learners begin by driving relatively slowly, and this is fine when driving along a dual carriageway. However, joining a dual carriageway from a slip road can call for firm acceleration. If your learner is not too confident with accelerating through the gears, wait until the skill has developed before attempting to join a dual carriageway from a slip road.

When overtaking, your learner will need to judge the length of their vehicle accurately. If they do not, there's a danger of cutting in too soon as they return to the left lane.

Remember

Vehicles ahead may want to turn right through the central reservation. Do not let your learner confuse their right signal and positioning in the right-hand lane as a sign that they're overtaking, when other clues (such as brake lights or a junction sign) show that they may be turning right.

Parking

See page 78

On their driving test, your learner may be asked to demonstrate their ability to park in a bay in a car park or in a space behind another parked car on the side of the road. See pages 78 to 80 for details of the driving-test requirements.

Remember

Whether parking in a car park or on the roadside, your learner should be able to position the car accurately, confidently and safely. You must ensure that your learner does not hit another vehicle while they're practising.

How you can help

When practising reverse parking on the side of the road, your learner will inevitably cause a temporary obstruction to any traffic flow. For this reason, choose a quiet location for practice.

To practise parking in a parking bay, you'll need to find a suitable car park where your learner can practise this manoeuvre. Avoid busy car parks and peak times of day. Try to find a parking bay that has an empty bay on either side, which will allow a greater margin for inaccurate steering. While your learner's vehicle control skills are developing, you can help by being their eyes and ears, watching out for other road users. As car control develops, you can let them become responsible for the safety aspects themselves.

As with other reverse manoeuvres, do not allow your learner to rely only on the car's mirrors while reversing.

What to expect

Parking calls for accuracy, control and judgement. Your learner may be weak in any or all of these skills. When parking in a parking bay, they should be able to reverse into a bay and drive out as well as drive into a bay and reverse out. Make sure they do not go beyond the edge of the bay, or pose a risk to people or property in the car park.

When they set about reverse parking on the side of the road, you can expect them to have trouble judging where to pull up in readiness to reverse into the space. This may result in pulling up too close alongside, or too far past, the parked car, or perhaps not far enough forward past the parking space.

Emergency stop

See page 81

Practising stopping the car as if there were an emergency provides valuable experience in reacting quickly and correctly while controlling the car under emergency conditions. Practising what to do in an emergency is the only way to help your learner to cope if a real situation ever arises.

How you can help

Find somewhere with very little traffic, a good road surface, and where screeching tyres will not cause a nuisance. Agree with your learner the signal to give and begin practising at low speeds. Progress to higher speeds only when your learner has gained sufficient control skills to cope. Also, make sure that you look around carefully before giving any signal to stop – do not rely on your additional mirror as you might miss something.

What to expect

The ADI will have given instruction in the use of the controls. If your vehicle has an anti-lock braking system fitted, there may be special instructions on how to achieve maximum braking. Be prepared for your learner to use excessive force when applying the brakes, which may cause

- skidding, accompanied by loud screeching and smoke from the tyres
- a severe jolt that could cause injury to your back or neck.

On giving the signal, brace yourself and prepare for a sudden rapid deceleration.

Independent driving and using a sat nav

See page 84

Learning to drive independently is an important part of preparing your learner

- for their driving test
- to drive after they've passed their driving test.

On their driving test, a learner will be asked to drive independently for around 20 minutes. Most candidates will be asked to follow directions from a sat nav provided by the examiner. The examiner will supply the sat nav and set the route, so it does not matter what make or model of sat nav you use while you're practising. One in 5 driving tests will not use a sat nav; the learner will need to follow traffic signs instead.

Learner drivers can come to rely on the direction they're given as a prompt to begin the MSM/PSL routine. If you remove the step-by-step directions, they'll need to think for themselves and plan ahead, exactly as they will when driving unaccompanied.

Remember

At first your learner may be unsure where to go, especially at complicated junctions. Give them help if they need it, but as they're approaching their driving test they should be thinking for themselves.

How you can help

To help your learner drive independently, you'll need to give them some practice at following directions from a sat nav. You can also ask them to follow the directions shown on road signs and give them the opportunity to think for themselves.

What to expect

At first, they may be so focused on thinking about the directions that they forget to signal or are late moving into the correct lane or road position. They may also overlook other important features, such as traffic lights, pedestrian crossings or road markings. You should be ready to step in if necessary. Once they start to think for themselves and plan ahead, they'll be better prepared for driving after they've passed their test.

Darkness

See page 87

Your learner needs to practise driving in the dark since this calls for a new set of skills. As well as knowing how and when to use the car's lights, they have to learn how to

- cope with poor visibility when light levels are low
- deal with the glare from the lights of other vehicles
- avoid dazzling other road users.

How you can help

Try to give your learner as much experience as possible of driving in the dark on a range of roads, such as well-lit urban roads, unlit rural roads and dual carriageways. When driving in the dark, show your learner

- how to use the anti-dazzle feature on the interior mirror
- how and when to dip the main-beam headlights to avoid dazzling others.

When driving on rural roads without footpaths, ask them to think about pedestrians.

- Where should they be walking?
- What if they're wearing dark clothing?

Could your learner cope?

Make sure they check The Highway Code for advice and rules on driving, parking, vehicle lighting and use of the horn at night.

What to expect

The bright lights of oncoming traffic can be difficult to cope with. If an approaching driver has forgotten to dip their headlights, your learner may be dazzled and unable to see the road ahead. Do not let them

- continue without reducing speed
- retaliate by using their headlights to dazzle the approaching driver.

Do not forget that vulnerable road users, such as cyclists, pedestrians and motorcyclists, may be very difficult to see in the dark.

Many people adapt easily to driving in the dark, but others find it very tiring. If your learner finds it tiring, be ready to end the practice session and take over the driving yourself.

Remember

In busy urban areas, lights from shops and street lamps can make it easy to miss traffic lights, crossing lights, vulnerable road users and so on. You're responsible for making sure that no mistakes are made.

Weather conditions

See page 90

Adverse weather conditions such as fog, frost, high winds and rain are all common driving conditions.

In more severe weather conditions of snow and ice, be guided by the advice of local travel experts to determine whether conditions are suitable for your learner.

How you can help

If the conditions are not severe, you should take opportunities for your learner to practise when possible. In bad weather, your learner needs to pay attention to how the conditions affect their

- speed and ability to stop
- use of windscreen wipers/demisters
- need to use dipped headlights.

Explain that, just because they may think they can see adequately during the day in dull, foggy or wet conditions, this does not mean their vehicle can be seen clearly by others. If in doubt, use dipped headlights for safety and visibility until conditions improve.

What to expect

Driving too close to the vehicle in front is a common mistake. Make sure that the 2-second rule is used, and that the gap is increased if conditions will affect the stopping distance. Front or rear fog lights may be used if fitted, but make sure they're turned off if conditions improve.

Also remember that anti-lock braking systems (ABS) do not replace the need for good driving skills. ABS prevents wheels from locking, so that steering control is retained, but vehicles can still skid because of ice, surface water or a loose road surface. Make sure that your learner fully understands this.

Fuel-efficient driving

See page 93

Your learner needs to understand that they can reduce exhaust emissions by driving in a fuel-efficient manner. They'll save money by using less fuel, and they'll improve their hazard awareness skills by looking and planning further ahead.

How you can help

The ADI should be able to explain the recommended driving techniques, which can also be found in 'The Official DVSA Guide to Driving – the essential skills'. Encourage your learner to practise these techniques.

Keeping a check on fuel consumption will show you the effect that driving in this manner can have. This may encourage you to adopt these techniques yourself.

To help your learner appreciate the issues that surround fuel-efficient driving, talk about the importance of

- good planning
- keeping tyres correctly inflated.

Remember

Harsh use of the accelerator and heavy braking significantly increases fuel consumption.

What to expect

Learners tend to drive more slowly than experienced drivers until their confidence builds. You can help your learner to understand that careful use of speed and an awareness of fuel consumption will help them continue to drive in a fuel-efficient manner. Encourage them to keep doing so.

Passengers and loads

See page 96

Your learner must understand the driver's responsibility when carrying passengers. They must be aware of the seat-belt regulations, details of which are in The Highway Code.

They must also understand the effect that a load can have on a vehicle's handling/braking and the importance of not overloading their vehicle. Help your learner develop good awareness of their responsibilities to prevent them from breaking the law.

How you can help

Letting your learner drive with passengers can be a valuable experience. If any are under 14 years, the driver is responsible for ensuring that they wear a seat belt or appropriate child restraint. Make sure that your learner is aware of this. It's also the driver's responsibility to stop anyone in the car from smoking if any passenger is under 18.

Use any opportunity to let your learner practise in a loaded vehicle; for example, when going on holiday. Discuss the way that extra weight can affect the vehicle and explain the importance of making sure that the load is secure and not sticking out dangerously.

See the vehicle handbook for advice on altering tyre pressures when carrying heavy loads.

What to expect

If the car is heavily loaded, its acceleration may be slower than normal. Make sure that your learner takes this into account when emerging from a side road, or moving off on an uphill gradient. Braking may also be affected – make sure that your learner understands this and recognises that they should allow themselves more time and a greater distance in which to stop the vehicle safely.

If you're carrying an animal such as a family pet in the car, it's important to keep it under control. Loose animals can be a serious distraction and could cause an incident.

Remember

If the car is filled with people, there's likely to be conversation. Make sure this does not distract either of you.

Security

See page 99

Your learner needs to be aware of the importance of security – not only of the vehicle and its contents, but also their own personal security. Information on vehicle safety can be obtained from your local crime prevention officer.

How you can help

When looking for a place to park the car, your learner may be preoccupied with the process of parking and not thinking about the security issues.

If they choose to park in a place that has a security risk, ask them whether they think they've chosen a safe place to park. If necessary, you should point out the risk. Make sure they understand the importance of not parking in poorly lit areas and not leaving any valuables on display.

If your vehicle is fitted with an immobiliser and/ or alarm, make sure your learner is familiar with its operation and that they use it whenever they park the car.

If you have a high-visibility security device, such as a steering-wheel lock, show your learner how to use it.

What to expect

If your learner is naturally security conscious, they'll happily take measures that cut down the risks. If not, you may have to nag them to understand that using a car makes them a potential target for car crime; it's in their own interest to safeguard themselves and their property.

Remember

Many car crimes are committed on service station forecourts when the driver leaves the car to pay for fuel. Alerting your learner to the risk may prevent them from becoming a victim.

Section three

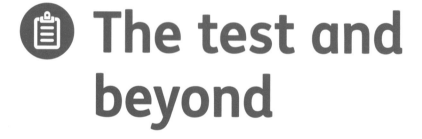

The test and beyond

In this section, you'll learn about

- deciding when you're ready for your test
- how to book your practical driving test
- what will happen on the day of your test
- the practical test
- your test result
- Pass Plus
- developing your driving skills.

Are you ready for your test?

You'll be ready for your practical test when you've ticked off all the key skills listed on the 'Driver's Record', not before.

The pass rate for the practical test is about 45%. Those learner drivers who pass first time do so because they've had plenty of professional instruction and practice. Make sure you're one of them.

Remember

Your instructor has the knowledge and experience to tell you when you're ready. You'll be ready when you can drive consistently well, with confidence and without assistance or guidance. If you cannot do this all the time, you're not ready to take your test.

Are you sure you're ready to drive on your own? Do not apply for your test too soon; wait until you're ready. It'll save you time and money.

It's important that, throughout your training, you've been learning the theory and putting it into practice when you drive – you need to do the 2 things in parallel. However, you'll need to take and pass a theory test before you can apply to take your practical driving test.

The theory test

There are 2 parts to the theory test: the first consists of multiple choice questions, and the second is a hazard perception test. Both parts are taken in the same session.

There are more than 175 theory test centres in Great Britain and 6 in Northern Ireland. Theory test sessions are available on weekdays, some evenings and some Saturdays.

You'll usually be able to get an appointment within about 2 weeks (a bit longer if you have special needs).

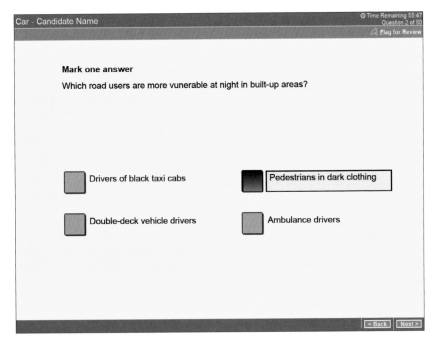

The multiple choice questions will be on a screen like this. To answer a question, you click on the answer you think is correct. If you're not sure of the correct answer, you can flag the question and return to it later.

You can find out where your local centre is from your instructor, online at **www.gov.uk** or by calling **0300 200 1122**.

More information about the theory test can found on our online learning portal; simply visit **dvsalearningzone.co.uk**

Or you can practise all the revision questions and hazard perception clips by downloading our award-winning 'The Official DVSA Theory Test Kit for Car Drivers' app. Scan this QR code for a link to your relevant app store.

When you pass your theory test, you'll be given a pass certificate. You have to quote the number on this certificate when you book your practical test, and you must bring the certificate with you when you take your practical test.

The theory test certificate is valid for 2 years. If you do not pass your practical test within that time, you'll have to take and pass another theory test before you can book your practical test.

When you drive on your practical test, your examiner will expect you to demonstrate what you learnt for your theory test.

I cannot read very well, so I'm worried about taking my test

If you have reading difficulties, there's a voiceover for the test, which may help. You may also be allowed extra time in some circumstances. You can select this option when you book your test online.

How will I know what to do on the hazard perception part of the test?

Once you've completed the multiple choice part of the test, and before you start the hazard perception part, you'll be shown a short tutorial video that explains how the test works and gives you a chance to see a sample clip. This will help you to understand what you're expected to do once the second part of the test starts.

Booking your practical driving test

How to book

You have all the boxes on your 'Driver's Record' completed, you've passed your theory test and you're ready to take your practical test.

You can book your test online or by telephone.

Online or by telephone You'll be given the date and time of your test immediately. You can book online at **www.gov.uk**

To book by telephone, call **0300 200 1122** Monday to Friday. If you're deaf and use a minicom machine, call **0300 200 1144**. If you're a Welsh speaker, call **0300 200 1133**.

You'll need to tell the operator what sort of test you want to book and provide

- your theory test pass certificate number
- your driver number (shown on your licence)
- your driving school code number (if you have it)
- your credit/debit card details. Please note that the person who books the test must be the card holder.

You may be asked if you can accept a test at short notice. Ask your instructor beforehand about this if you would need to use their car. You'll be given a booking number and sent an appointment letter within a few days.

Apply well in advance of when you want to take your test. At test centres in Wales, you can take the test in the Welsh language. Please indicate your choice when booking.

Disabilities or special circumstances

Whichever way you book your test, you need to tell DVSA if you have a disability or if there are other special circumstances; for example, whether you

- are deaf or have serious hearing difficulties
- are in any way restricted in your movements
- have any disability that may affect your driving.

However serious your disability is, you'll still take the same driving test as every other test candidate, but more time will be allowed for the test. This is so that your examiner can talk to you about your disability and any adaptations fitted to your vehicle. For further information, visit **www.gov.uk**.

Tell us if you have reading difficulties or a learning disability. Your examiner will understand and will discuss with you alternative ways to complete the independent driving part of the test.

If any of these apply to you, remember to say so when you book your test. If you're deaf or have severe hearing problems, you're allowed to bring a signer. (This can be your instructor.) The signer must be 16 years or over.

How much does the test cost?

Your instructor should be able to tell you, or you can find out on **www.gov.uk** or by calling **0300 200 1122**.

Can I take my test on a weekend or in the evening?

At some test centres, you can take a test on a Saturday or Sunday, or on a weekday evening. The fees at these times are higher than those for tests during normal working hours on weekdays. Evening tests are available during the summer months only.

How do I change or cancel my test?

You can change or cancel your test online at **www.gov.uk** or by calling the booking office on **0300 200 1122**. (You may even be able to switch to an earlier date.)

You must give at least 3 clear working days' notice, not counting the day DVSA receives your request and the day of the test. (Saturday is counted as a working day.) If you do not give enough notice, you'll lose your fee. (Short-notice rebooking is permitted in exceptional circumstances – see **www.gov.uk** for details.)

The day of your test

Make sure that you arrive for your test in good time and try to relax. You need to bring the correct documents with you and ensure that the vehicle you'll be driving is suitable for the driving test.

Documents

When you arrive at the test centre, you need to have with you

- your provisional driving licence
- your theory test pass certificate
- your valid passport, if your licence does not show your photograph. (Your passport does not have to be British.) No other form of identification is acceptable in England, Wales or Scotland. Other documents may, however, be acceptable in Northern Ireland; please check **nidirect.gov.uk/motoring**

Your examiner will not be able to conduct the test if you cannot produce one of these licences

- a provisional driving licence issued in Great Britain or Northern Ireland, or a full GB or NI licence giving the provisional entitlement
- an EC/EEA licence if you want to take a test for a category not covered by your full EC/EEA licence.

If you have a full driving licence that was issued in another country but is not eligible for exchange for a GB licence, you must have a GB provisional licence.

All documents must be original – DVSA cannot accept photocopies.

Your test vehicle

Make sure that the vehicle you're going to drive during the test is

- legally roadworthy and has a current MOT test certificate if it needs one
- mechanically sound and all equipment required by law is fitted and working correctly; for example, the speedometer must show mph and km/h. In some cars, the spare wheel is a space saver intended for temporary use only. The vehicle is not suitable for use on a driving test if a space-saver wheel is being used
- fully covered by insurance for its present use and for you to drive – your examiner will ask you to sign a declaration that your insurance is in order before you take your test.

A hire car can only be used for the driving test if it's fitted with dual controls. Any vehicle used for the test should also have

- valid vehicle tax
- L plates (or, if you wish, D plates if you're taking your test in Wales) displayed to the front and rear of the vehicle – do not fix them to the windscreen or back window as both you and your examiner should have a clear view of the road
- seat belts – make sure they're clean and work properly
- head restraints fitted ('slip-on' head restraints are not permissible on test)
- an additional interior rear-view mirror for the examiner to use.

Can I take my test in an automatic car?

You can, but if you pass you'll get a full licence only to drive an automatic. There's sometimes some confusion about what's classed as an automatic. For clarity, vehicles with 3 pedals (accelerator, brake and clutch) are classed as manual; vehicles with 2 pedals are classed as automatics.

The controls, seating, equipment and any other objects in the vehicle must be arranged so that they do not interfere with the conduct of the test. A dual accelerator (if fitted) must be removed before the test.

You will not be able to take your test if your vehicle is not suitable; for example, if it

- has no clear view to the rear, other than by use of the exterior mirrors
- has only a driver's seat
- has more than 8 passenger seats or is over 3.5 tonnes in weight
- does not have seat belts or head restraints fitted to the front seats
- has been subject to a manufacturer's recall but you do not have a certificate showing that the work has been carried out
- is carrying a load
- is towing a trailer (see page 191).

If you're using a left-hand-drive car, take special care and make full use of your mirrors.

Remember

If you overlook any of these points, your test will be cancelled and you'll lose your fee. Make sure that your vehicle is suitable for the test well in advance.

Adapted vehicles

If you pass your test in a motor car that has been specifically adapted for your disability, your licence will restrict you to driving vehicles fitted with the necessary adaptations.

The practical test

Try to relax and drive as you've been driving during your lessons and practice.

Your examiner wants you to do well and will try to help you relax. If you want to talk during the test, that will not be a problem – your examiner will talk with you but might not say too much because they do not want to distract you from your driving. Do not worry if you make a mistake; keep calm and concentrate on your driving for the rest of the test. Unless it's a serious or dangerous fault, you will not fail on this unless you make the same mistake a number of times.

You'll pass if you can show your examiner that you can drive safely and demonstrate, through your driving, that you have a thorough knowledge of the rules of The Highway Code and the theory of driving safely.

Does the standard of test vary?

No, all examiners are trained to assess tests to the same standard.
The test routes are designed to include a range of typical road and traffic
conditions and the examiners are closely supervised to make sure they
follow the national standard. A senior examiner sits in on some tests
to make sure the examiner is assessing the standard of your driving
properly. If this happens on your test, do not worry – they will not be
looking at you, so just carry on as if they were not there.

Can anyone accompany me on the test?

Yes, we encourage this. The examiner will ask you if you would like your
instructor, or anyone else (preferably the person who trained you to
drive) to accompany you on test and be there for the result and end-of-
test feedback.

It can be helpful to take your instructor with you. Pass or fail, your
instructor can discuss your test with you and identify any further training
you might need.

Anyone who goes with you must be 16 or over and wear a seat belt, but
they must not take any part in the test.

Your driving instructor should be preparing you to drive alone after you've
passed the test, so you should already be learning the skills you need to do
so and be able to make decisions for yourself. Once you've passed your test,
you'll need to navigate roads safely, often dealing with distractions such as
passengers and music.

Throughout the test, your examiner will be watching how you drive and how
you put into practice the things you learnt for your theory test.

You must satisfy them that you've fully understood all aspects, especially

- alertness and concentration
- courtesy and consideration
- care in the use of the controls to reduce mechanical wear and tear
- awareness of stopping distances, speed limits and safety margins in
  all conditions
- hazard awareness

- correct action concerning pedestrians and other vulnerable road users
- dealing with other types of vehicle in the correct manner
- road and traffic signs.

The test lasts for about 40 minutes. The route will have been selected to include as many different road and traffic conditions as possible.

Your examiner will give you directions clearly and in good time, but if you're not sure about anything, just ask. Your examiner understands that you might be nervous and will not mind explaining again.

Other elements in the test

Apart from general driving, your test will include the following elements:

Eyesight test Before you get into your car, your examiner will point out a vehicle at a suitable distance and ask you to read its number plate. You must satisfy them that you can read it, as detailed on page 11. If you need glasses or contact lenses to read the number plate, that's fine, but you must wear them during the test and whenever you drive.

If you cannot speak English or have difficulty reading, you may copy down what you see.

If your answer is incorrect, your examiner will measure the exact distance and repeat the test. If you fail the eyesight test, your test will go no further.

Safety checks Your examiner will ask you

- one 'tell me' question at the beginning of your test, before you start driving. This is where you explain how you'd carry out a safety task
- one 'show me' question while you're driving; for example, show me how to wash the windscreen using the car controls (see page 31).

Special exercises You'll be asked to carry out one of 3 possible reversing manoeuvres

- parallel park at the side of the road (see page 78)
- park in a bay (see page 79)
- stop and reverse on the right-hand side of the road (see pages 68 to 69).

Independent driving All practical driving tests include approximately 20 minutes of independent driving, when you'll be asked to drive by either

- following directions from a sat nav, or
- following traffic signs towards a destination.

This part of the test will enable your examiner to assess how you manage traffic and road systems on your own, and show that you have the skills to be a safe novice driver.

Your examiner will also ask you to pull up on the left several times during the test. This is to demonstrate your ability to stop and move away

- safely
- on a gradient
- from behind a parked vehicle
- while in full control of your car.

Emergency stop You may be asked to carry out an emergency stop. (One in 3 tests includes an emergency-stop exercise.)

How the examiner records faults

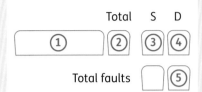

1. **Driving fault** A less serious fault, but an accumulation of these may result in failure

2. **Area total** The number of driving faults made in one area

3. **Serious fault** Committing one of these will result in failure

4. **Dangerous fault** Committing one of these will result in failure

5. **Overall total** The total number of driving faults made in all areas during the test.

How your driving test is assessed

Your examiner is looking for evidence that you have the required skills, knowledge and attitude to be a safe driver.

Throughout your driving test, your examiner will assess your driving and will complete a report, which is used to provide you with feedback at the end of the test.

You'll fail your test if you commit a serious or dangerous fault. You'll also fail if you commit more than 15 driving faults.

The examiner will use the following criteria

Driving fault Less serious, but has been assessed as such because of circumstances at that particular time. An accumulation of more than 15 driving faults will result in failure.

Serious fault Recorded when a potentially dangerous incident has occurred or a habitual driving fault indicates a serious weakness in a candidate's driving.

Dangerous fault Recorded when a fault is assessed as having caused actual danger during the test.

Guidance after the test

After the test, pass or fail, you'll be offered feedback on your driving performance and an explanation of your driving-test report.

The Data Protection Act prevents your instructor from talking to your examiner about your practical test without your permission.

Having your instructor in the car will give them the opportunity to support your ongoing learning and development. We encourage you to let your instructor see your test and listen to the test result and feedback.

If you have not passed, your instructor will have a better understanding of the reasons for this. They will then be able to address the specific weaknesses you've shown during the drive through further training before your next test.

If you've passed, your instructor will be better placed to advise you about your ongoing development as a new driver.

Fuel-efficient driving

Fuel-efficient driving is a recognised and proven style of driving that contributes to road safety while reducing fuel consumption and emissions.

At the end of the test, the examiner may remind you to discuss fuel-efficient driving with your instructor and the benefits it brings.

Your test result

If you do not pass

Your driving is not up to the standard required. You made mistakes that could have caused danger on the road.

Your examiner will help you by

- giving you a driving-test report form. This will show all the faults marked during the test
- explaining briefly why you have not passed.

Listen to your examiner carefully. They'll be able to help you by pointing out the aspects of your driving that you need to improve.

Study the driving-test report. It will include notes to help you understand how the examiner marks the form. You may then find it helpful to look at the relevant sections in this book.

Show your copy of the report to your instructor, who will advise and help you to correct the faults. Listen to your instructor's advice carefully and get as much practice as you can. You cannot take another test for at least 10 days.

Right of appeal You'll obviously be disappointed if you do not pass your driving test. Although your examiner's decision cannot be changed, if you think your test was not carried out according to the regulations, you have the right to appeal. If you live in England and Wales, you have 6 months after the issue of the Statement of Failure in which to appeal (Magistrates' Courts Act 1952 Ch. 55 part VII, Sect. 104).

If you live in Scotland, you have 21 days in which to appeal (Sheriff Court, Scotland Act of Sederunt (Statutory Appeals) 1981).

If you pass

Well done! You've shown that you can drive safely and confidently. Your examiner will give you a copy of the driving-test report, which will show any driving faults that have been marked during the test.

Your examiner will then ask for your provisional licence so that the details can be recorded.

Once the details have been taken, your examiner will keep your provisional licence and it will be securely destroyed. You'll be given a pass certificate as proof of success and your new licence will be sent out to you.

If you do not want to surrender your licence you do not have to, and there will be certain circumstances when this is not possible – for example, if you've changed your name.

In these cases, you'll have to send your provisional licence, together with your pass certificate and the appropriate fee, to DVLA and it will send you your full licence. You must do this within 2 years or you'll have to take your test again.

Look at the test report carefully and discuss it with your instructor. It includes notes to help you understand how the examiner marks the form.

You may then find it helpful to look at the relevant sections in this book to help you overcome those weaknesses noted during your test.

Special rules under the New Drivers Act apply for the first 2 years after you've passed your test.

What can I drive with my full category B licence?

You can drive vehicles up to 3,500 kg maximum authorised mass (MAM) with up to 8 passenger seats (with a trailer up to 750 kg).

You can also tow heavier trailers if the total MAM of the vehicle and trailer is not more than 3,500 kg.

You can drive motor tricycles with a power output higher than 15 kW if you're over 21 years old.

In addition, you can drive

- a light van of up to 3.5 tonnes MAM
- alternatively fuelled vehicles that weigh up to 4.25 tonnes, provided you complete a minimum of 5 hours of additional relevant training (see National Register of LGV Instructors (**lgvinstructorregister.com**) and the National Vocational Driving Instructors Register (**lgvregister.org.uk**) for training providers).

If your test vehicle had automatic transmission, you can only drive category B vehicles that have automatic transmission.

Be aware that different speed limits apply to vehicles weighing more than 2 tonnes maximum laden weight.

New Drivers Act

Your licence will be revoked if you receive 6 or more penalty points as a result of offences you commit within 2 years of passing your first practical test. This includes any offences you may have committed before passing your test.

 Remember

You'll get a minimum of 3 penalty points for speeding – 2 speeding offences means 6 points.

If you wish to continue driving, you'll have to reapply for a provisional licence. You'll then have to drive as a learner until you pass the theory and practical driving tests again. This applies even if you pay by fixed penalty.

For more information, see **www.gov.uk**

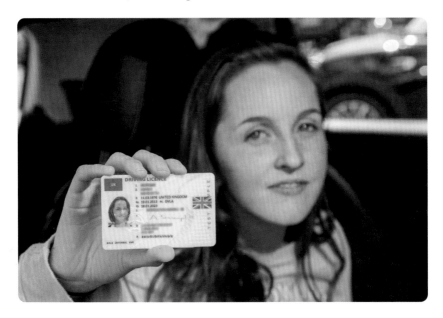

Pass Plus

Pass Plus is a training scheme for new drivers. Its aim is to improve your driving skills and make you a safer driver. It can also lead to insurance discounts.

The scheme has been designed by the Driver and Vehicle Standards Agency (DVSA), with the help of motor insurers and driving instructors, to develop your skills and knowledge in areas in which you may have limited experience.

As an indicator of its effectiveness, a survey of practical test candidates (carried out by ORC International for DVSA) showed that, among those who had taken Pass Plus

- 93% felt more confident on the road
- 89% considered that their driving skills had improved.

This was as a result of taking the course.

Three ways to find out more

1 Visit **www.gov.uk**

2 Email **passplus@dvsa.gov.uk**

3 Telephone **0115 936 6504**

What are the benefits?

Pass Plus will benefit you by

- enabling you to gain quality driving experience safely
- helping you to become a more skilful driver
- teaching you how to develop a positive driving style that's both enjoyable and safe

- reducing your risk of being involved in a road crash
- saving you money on your car insurance premiums.*

* Subject to status. Candidates are advised to check available discounts with participating insurance companies.

Pass Plus consists of a minimum of 6 hours' training, and the emphasis is on developing your practical driving skills. There's no test at the end. Instead, you'll be assessed throughout: you must cover all the modules to complete the training.

When you've successfully completed Pass Plus, you'll have demonstrated that you

- have developed your existing skills
- have acquired new skills and knowledge
- can drive safely in conditions not included in the driving test
- understand how you can reduce the risk of having a road traffic incident
- can maintain a courteous and considerate attitude to other road users.

Enjoy the course!

Saving money on your car insurance should bring a smile to your face.

Developing your driving skills

Motorway driving

As a learner, you may have been able to experience motorway driving (see page 21, 76 to 77). If you have not, it's important that you understand the rules and regulations before you drive on your own on a motorway.

If you take Pass Plus, one of the modules relates solely to motorway driving. Alternatively, you can ask your instructor for motorway driving lessons. Either of these will give you valuable experience of motorway driving.

Further training

Do you feel ready for the next level? If so, contact one of the organisations below.

DVSA has approved and monitors advanced driving tests offered by

IAM RoadSmart
Telephone
0300 303 1134
iamroadsmart.com

DIAmond Advanced Motorists
Telephone
020 8253 0120
advancedmotoring.co.uk

RoSPA Advanced Drivers and Riders (RoADAR)
Telephone
0121 248 2099
roadar.org.uk

Section four

 **Other tests**

In this section, you'll learn about

- the category B+E trailer test
- retests for those who have lost their licence.

Towing a trailer

You must have a full car* driving licence before you can tow any trailer or caravan. The key factor that determines what licence you need is the maximum authorised mass (MAM)** of the car and trailer.

If you passed your test before 1 January 1997, you can drive a car and trailer or caravan combination of up to 8.25 tonnes MAM.

If you passed your test after 1 January 1997, you can

- drive a vehicle of up to 3.5 tonnes (or 3,500 kg) MAM, towing a trailer of up to 750 kg MAM
- tow a trailer over 750 kg MAM as long as the combined weight of the trailer and towing vehicle is no more than 3,500 kg.

If you passed your test after 19 January 2013, you can tow

- small trailers weighing no more than 750 kg
- a trailer over 750 kg as long as the combined weight of the trailer and towing vehicle is no more than 3,500 kg MAM.

If you wish to drive larger car and trailer combinations, you'll normally have to take a further test (category B+E). Information about towing is available at **www.gov.uk**

Further information

Detailed information and advice about towing trailers can be found in *The Official DVSA Guide to Driving – the essential skills*, which can be purchased from good bookshops or by calling **0333 200 2401**.

Useful information on towing can also be found on the following websites

- **ntta.co.uk** (National Trailer and Towing Association Ltd)
- **caravanclub.co.uk**
- **campingandcaravanningclub.co.uk**

* A car includes any four-wheeled vehicle with a MAM of up to 3.5 tonnes that has no more than 8 passenger seats.

** The MAM is the maximum permissible weight, also known as the gross vehicle weight.

If I do not fully load the trailer, can I tow a bigger one?

No, the size of trailer you can tow is dependent on the MAM, not the actual weight when loaded.

Do I have to take a theory test?

No, you've already passed a car theory test. There's no additional theory test for drivers towing trailers in category B+E.

Key towing skills

You should consistently drive to the level detailed on pages 25 to 100; that is, to at least the levels shown in the 'Driver's Record', the standard required to pass a car test. There are, however, some differences and these are explained here.

Safety checks

You need to know how to carry out checks on the condition of the trailer body, check that any doors are secure, and know how to load and secure a load to the trailer. At the beginning of the test, the examiner will ask you to explain or demonstrate 5 separate safety checks.

Mirrors

You should know how to use additional mirrors and take relevant observation to compensate for the restricted view caused by large trailers and caravans.

Other traffic

You should always show consideration for other road users by pulling up safely, when necessary, to allow others to pass and avoid the build-up of queues of traffic behind you.

Turning the vehicle around

You need to know how to turn the vehicle and trailer around so you can travel in the opposite direction; for example, using a roundabout or side roads.

Reversing

There will be an off-road reversing exercise that's normally carried out at the beginning of the test. You'll need to be able to reverse the car and trailer on a predetermined course to enter a restricted opening and then stop so that the extreme rear of the trailer is within a clearly defined area.

Emergency stop

There's no emergency-stop exercise for the B+E test.

Uncoupling and recoupling

You'll also need to be able to uncouple and recouple your car and trailer. This is normally carried out at the end of the test (see pages 200 to 203).

Practising (B+E)

When you practise, you **MUST**

- display L plates to the front of the car and the rear of the trailer. These must be clearly visible. You may use D plates in Wales if you wish
- be accompanied by a person who's at least 21 years old and holds a full EC/EEA driving licence for category B+E (they must have held this for the past 3 years).

You should also practise reversing and uncoupling/recoupling your car and trailer. You'll be asked to do both these exercises as part of your test.

You should practise in all sorts of traffic conditions and on as many different roads as you can, including motorways.

Your trailer **MUST** be laden for the test (see page 195), so you're advised to practise with a laden trailer.

Practise turning left and right, taking into consideration the extra length of the unit. Be aware of your trailer, especially when taking sharp turns.

Booking and taking your test

Book your test as you would a car test (see page 172). However, be sure to make it clear that you want to take a B+E test.

The test can take place only at test centres for drivers of lorries and buses, where there's a manoeuvring area. To find out where these are, ask your trainer, call **0300 200 1122** or visit **www.gov.uk**

Also, as the test is longer, there's a higher fee.

Documents

Make sure that you have your full licence with you and that it's signed. If your licence does not show your photograph, you must bring your passport. (Your passport does not have to be British.)

Only licences issued in Great Britain or Northern Ireland are acceptable. Your examiner cannot conduct your test if you cannot produce the correct documents.

If you do not have the correct documents or you forget to bring them with you, your test will be cancelled and you'll lose your fee.

Your test vehicle

The vehicle you intend to drive during your test should satisfy all the requirements given on pages 176 to 177 for those taking a car test. The L plates need to be displayed to the front of your car and the rear of your trailer. In addition, the vehicle should have an audible or visible warning device to confirm that the trailer indicator lights are operating.

The trailer being used for the test **MUST**

- have a closed box body
- be laden in accordance with the rules that can be found at **www.gov.uk**

Your test will be cancelled and you can lose your fee if your vehicle does not meet the rules.

Vehicle–trailer combinations should be fitted with nearside and offside externally mounted mirrors for use by the examiner, and the car and trailer together must be capable of 62.5 mph (100 km/h).

Trailer loads must be either bagged aggregate or an intermediate bulk container (IBC) filled with water.

Your test

Your test will include the following parts:

Eyesight test Before you get into your car, your examiner will point out a vehicle at a suitable distance and ask you to read its number plate. You must satisfy them that you can read the number plate as detailed on page 11. If you need glasses or contact lenses to read the number plate, that's fine, but you must wear them during the test and whenever you drive.

If you cannot speak English or have difficulty reading, you may copy down what you see.

If your answer is incorrect, your examiner will measure the exact distance and repeat the test. If you fail the eyesight test, your driving test will go no further.

Additional exterior mirrors must be fitted for use by the examiner.

Safety-check questions The examiner will ask you to explain or demonstrate 5 separate safety checks. (See annex 3 for the official car and trailer (B+E) safety questions.)

The drive This will be approximately one hour long. It will include a wide variety of roads and traffic conditions, including roads carrying two-way traffic, dual carriageways and, where possible, one-way systems and motorways.

Your examiner will expect you to drive at least to the standard that you demonstrated during your car test.

However, during the drive you will not be asked to

- carry out an emergency-stop exercise
- reverse park.

Make sure that you negotiate all hazards and junctions safely by using good, all-round observation.

All practical driving tests include approximately 10 minutes of independent driving, during which you'll be asked to drive by following signs or a series of verbal directions, or a combination of both.

Reversing exercise This normally takes place before you leave the test centre but might be carried out at the end of the test. For full details of the reversing exercise, see pages 198 to 199.

Uncoupling and recoupling exercise For full details of the uncoupling and recoupling exercise, see pages 200 to 203.

The reversing exercise

The reversing exercise for this test will usually take place before you leave the test centre. You'll have to demonstrate that you can manoeuvre your car and trailer in a restricted space and stop at a specified point.

To carry out this part of the test, you should be able to reverse your car and trailer in a restricted space.

Your examiner will ask you to drive forward before you begin to reverse.

You should be able to do this inside a clearly defined area

- under control and in reasonable time
- with good observation
- with reasonable accuracy.

Your examiner will show you a diagram of the manoeuvring area and explain what's required. The size of the reversing area will be set out according to the size of your car and trailer together as a unit

- cone A1 is positioned 1 metre (just over 3 feet) into the area from the boundary line
- distance A to A1 is one-and-a-half times the width of the widest part of the unit
- A to B is twice the length of the car and trailer
- the overall length of the manoeuvring area will be 4 times the length of the car and trailer

- the width of the bay will be one-and-a-half times the widest part of the unit
- the length of the bay will be equal to the length of the car and trailer, up to a maximum of 12 metres. If the length of the car and trailer exceeds 12 metres, the bay will be set at 12 metres.

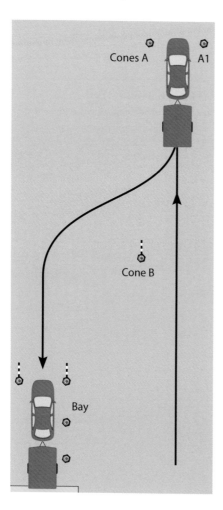

Cones A · A1

Cone B

Bay

Tips from the experts

Approach cones A and A1 in a straight line and make sure that you stop at the cones; do not go too fast and go past them.

Turn the steering wheel the correct way as you start to reverse.

Keep in full control; do not let your wheel go over the yellow boundary or allow any part of your car to hit any of the cones or poles.

Use good all-round observation throughout the manoeuvre.

Make sure that you stop so that the rear of your car and trailer is within the yellow box.

What to expect on test

You'll be asked to

- drive forward and stop at a fixed point with the extreme front of your car level with, and in between, the cones A and A1
- reverse so that you pass cone B on the offside of your car
- stop so that the extreme rear of your trailer is within the painted yellow box at the end of the bay.

Uncoupling and recoupling

You'll need to be able to uncouple the car and trailer, park the car and then recouple the two safely. You need to gain the skills to do this safely before you drive with a trailer on your own.

When uncoupling, you first of all need to find a safe place with firm and level ground on which to carry out the procedure. Then you should

- ensure that the brakes are applied on both the car and the trailer (various parking mechanisms are fitted to trailers; you should consult the manufacturer's handbook to ensure that you operate yours safely)
- ensure that the jockey wheel, legs or other devices provided for supporting the trailer after uncoupling are lowered correctly. If there's any risk, strong planks or metal load spreaders should be used to distribute the weight
- disconnect the electrical lines and stow them away safely
- remove any fitted stabilising equipment
- remove any safety chain or coupling and move the car clear of the trailer.

When hitching the trailer, check that the coupling is secure. You could do this by either lifting the hitch or winding the jockey wheel down onto the ground until it lifts the hitch.

When recoupling, you should treat the trailer as a new trailer that you have not used before. You should

- ensure the brakes are correctly applied to the trailer
- move the car so that the trailer can be safely and easily coupled to it, and apply the parking brake
- attach the trailer to the car and check that the coupling is secure by lift testing the hitch (see photos).
- attach any safety chain or breakaway cable
- fit any necessary stabilising equipment
- connect the electrical lines
- ensure that the wheels, legs or other supporting devices are raised and secured safely
- check the operation of the lights and indicators, and make sure the correct number plate is fitted
- release the trailer brake, ensuring that the car's parking brake is firmly applied.

What to expect on test

You'll normally be asked to uncouple and recouple your car and trailer at the test centre at the end of the test.

Your examiner will ask you to stop where there's safe and level ground and then uncouple your car from the trailer. You'll then be asked to park the car alongside the trailer before realigning the car with the trailer and recoupling the two. Your examiner will expect you to make sure that the

- coupling is secure
- lights and indicators are operating
- trailer brake is released.

If you use a vehicle with automatic transmission for your B+E test, when you pass, you'll be licensed to use only vehicles with automatic transmission when towing under B+E regulations.

When uncoupling or recoupling, make sure the brake is correctly applied before you start.

Tips from the experts

Make sure that you carry out the procedure in the correct sequence, and that you can do it confidently and without hesitating.

When uncoupling, make sure you've applied the brakes to both the car and trailer before you start and do not release the trailer coupling without the wheels or legs being lowered.

Do not try to move forward until the whole uncoupling procedure has been completed.

When recoupling, make sure that the brakes are applied on the trailer and that you use good all-round observation as you reverse.

Do not try to move away without raising the wheels or legs and checking the lights, indicators, safety chain and trailer brake release.

Make sure that the jockey wheel is lowered after uncoupling and then raised and secured safely when recoupling.

What can I drive with my B+E licence?

You can drive a vehicle with a MAM of 3,500 kg with a trailer.

The size of the trailer depends on the BE 'valid from' date shown on your licence. If the date is

- before 19 January 2013, you can tow any size trailer
- on or after 19 January 2013, you can tow a trailer with a MAM of up to 3,500 kg.

Retest for those who have lost their licence

Losing your licence

If you lose your licence after being convicted of a driving offence, you may have to take a normal-length or extended driving test before you can recover your full licence.

The court can impose the following penalties

- an extended driving test for anyone convicted of a dangerous driving offence (this is an obligatory penalty)
- an extended driving test for anyone convicted of other offences involving obligatory disqualification
- a normal-length driving test for other endorsable offences.

If you've been given one of these penalties, you can apply for a provisional licence at the end of the disqualification period.

If your licence has been revoked under the New Drivers Act (see page 186), you'll also have to apply for a new provisional licence.

Provisional licence

The normal rules for provisional licence-holders apply

- you must be supervised by a person who's at least 21 years old and who has held a full driving licence for the category of vehicle being driven for the past 3 years
- the car must display L plates (or D plates in Wales) to the front and rear
- learner driver conditions apply to driving on the motorway (see page 76).

You'll have to pass the theory test before you can apply to take your practical driving test again. You should study the training materials before you take the test (see pages 15 to 16).

Once you've passed the theory test, you can then apply to take your practical test.

Extended test

An extended test covers a wide variety of roads, usually including dual carriageways. This test is marked and assessed at the same level as a normal practical test, but it's more demanding because more time is devoted to normal driving. Make sure that you're ready.

Remember

The extended test lasts about 70 minutes. This is half an hour longer than the standard practical car test.

You're advised to take suitable instruction from an instructor.

You have to pay a higher fee for this test because of the longer duration.

What to expect on test

In addition to the longer drive detailed above, your test will include all the exercises included in the normal test.

You'll be asked to carry out one of 3 possible reversing manoeuvres

- parallel park at the side of the road (see page 78)
- park in a bay (see page 79)
- stop on the right-hand side of the road (see pages 68 to 69).

You'll also be asked to carry out an emergency stop during the test.

There will be approximately 20 minutes of independent driving, during which you'll be asked to drive by following directions from a sat nav provided and set by the examiner. One in 5 driving tests will not use a sat nav; you'll need to follow traffic signs instead.

Your examiner will watch you and, in addition to the normal observations detailed throughout this book, will take account of your ability to concentrate for the duration of the test and your attitude to other road users.

Annex one
Private practice record

When you go out driving with a friend or relative, DVSA would encourage you to record the type of driving experience that you've gained.

Expect over 40 hours of instruction and a further 20 or more practising with a suitable accompanying driver before you're ready to pass your practical test and drive on your own. People with the most experience on all kinds of roads in all conditions have fewer crashes. Clock these up with your ADI and accompanying driver before or as soon as you can after your test.

You can use these forms to record what you did by ticking the appropriate boxes. You'll probably tick several for each drive; for example, it may have been light when you started to drive but dark by the time you finished.

Visit **www.gov.uk** for further information and to download copies of these forms.

Date										
Wet roads										
Snow/ice										
Darkness										
Dual carriageway										
Country roads										
Town and city										
Independent driving										
Comments										

Date																								
Wet roads																								
Snow/ice																								
Darkness																								
Dual carriageway																								
Country roads																								
Town and city																								
Independent driving																								
Comments																								

Note:

Motorways. Before passing your test, you can only practise driving on a motorway if you're accompanied by an ADI, in a car fitted with dual controls. Motorways have a great safety record, but they can be unnerving at first.

Country roads. Practising on country roads is important as these are the roads where most crashes happen.

Annex two
Official car safety questions

'Tell me' questions

1. **Tell me how you'd check that the brakes are working before starting a journey.**

   Brakes should not feel spongy or slack. Brakes should be tested as you set off. Vehicle should not pull to one side.

2. **Tell me where you'd find the information for the recommended tyre pressures for this car and how tyre pressures should be checked.**

   Manufacturer's guide, use a reliable pressure gauge, check and adjust pressures when tyres are cold, do not forget spare tyre, remember to refit valve caps.

3. **Tell me how you make sure your head restraint is correctly adjusted so it provides the best protection in the event of a crash.**

   The head restraint should be adjusted so the rigid part of the head restraint is at least as high as the eye or top of the ears, and as close to the back of the head as is comfortable. Note: some restraints might not be adjustable.

4. **Tell me how you'd check the tyres to ensure that they have sufficient tread depth and that their general condition is safe to use on the road.**

   No cuts and bulges, 1.6 mm of tread depth across the central three-quarters of the breadth of the tyre, and around the entire outer circumference of the tyre.

5. **Tell me how you'd check that the headlights and tail lights are working. You do not need to exit the vehicle.**

   Explain you'd operate the switch (turn on ignition if necessary), then walk round vehicle (as this is a 'tell me' question, you do not need to physically check the lights).

6. **Tell me how you'd know if there was a problem with your anti-lock braking system.**

Warning light should illuminate if there's a fault with the anti-lock braking system.

7. **Tell me how you'd check the direction indicators are working. You do not need to exit the vehicle.**

Explain you'd operate the switch (turn on ignition if necessary), and then walk round vehicle (as this is a 'tell me' question, you do not need to physically check the lights).

8. **Tell me how you'd check the brake lights are working on this car.**

Explain you'd operate the brake pedal, make use of reflections in windows or doors, or ask someone to help.

9. **Tell me how you'd check the power-assisted steering is working before starting a journey.**

If the steering becomes heavy, the system may not be working properly. Before starting a journey, 2 simple checks can be made.

Gentle pressure on the steering wheel, maintained while the engine is started, should result in a slight but noticeable movement as the system begins to operate. Alternatively, turning the steering wheel just after moving off will give an immediate indication that the power assistance is functioning.

10. **Tell me how you'd switch on the rear fog lights and explain when you'd use it/them. You do not need to exit the vehicle.**

Operate switch (turn on dipped headlights and ignition if necessary). Check warning light is on. Explain use.

11. **Tell me how you switch your headlight from dipped to main beam and explain how you'd know the main beam is on.**

Operate switch (with ignition or engine on if necessary), check with main beam warning light.

12. **Open the bonnet and tell me how you'd check that the engine has sufficient oil.**

Identify dipstick/oil level indicator, describe check of oil level against the minimum and maximum markers.

13. **Open the bonnet and tell me how you'd check that the engine has sufficient engine coolant.**

    Identify high- and low-level markings on header tank where fitted or radiator filler cap, and describe how to top up to correct level.

14. **Open the bonnet and tell me how you'd check that you have a safe level of hydraulic brake fluid.**

    Identify reservoir, check level against high and low markings.

> You need to open the bonnet and tell the examiner how you'd do the check if you're asked question 12, 13 or 14.

'Show me' questions

1. **When it's safe to do so, can you show me how you wash and clean the rear windscreen?**

2. **When it's safe to do so, can you show me how you wash and clean the front windscreen?**

3. **When it's safe to do so, can you show me how you'd switch on your dipped headlights?**

4. **When it's safe to do so, can you show me how you'd set the rear demister?**

5. **When it's safe to do so, can you show me how you'd operate the horn?**

6. **When it's safe to do so, can you show me how you'd demist the front windscreen?**

7. **When it's safe to do so, can you show me how you'd open and close the side window?**

Annex three

Official car and trailer (B+E) safety questions

1. **Open the bonnet, identify where the brake fluid reservoir is and tell me how you would check that you have a safe level of hydraulic brake fluid.**

   Identify reservoir, check level against high/low markings.

2. **Show me how you would check that the direction indicators are working.**

   Applying the indicators or hazard warning switch and checking functioning of all indicators.

3. **Tell me the main safety factors involved in loading this vehicle.**

   The load should be distributed evenly throughout the trailer. Heavy items should be loaded as low as possible so that they are mainly over the axles. Bulkier, lighter items should be distributed to give a suitable 'nose weight' at the towing coupling. The nose weight should never exceed the vehicle manufacturer's specifications.

4. **Tell me the main safety factors involved in securing a load on this vehicle.**

   Any load must be carried so that it does not endanger other road users. It must be securely stowed within the size and weight limits for the vehicle. The load needs to be secure so that it cannot move or fall from the vehicle when cornering or braking.

5. **Show me how you would check that your vehicle and trailer doors are secure.**

   Physical checks should be made to ensure that windows, roof light and all doors, including cargo doors, are properly closed.

6. **Tell me how you would check the tyres to ensure that they have sufficient tread depth and that their general condition is safe to use on the road.**

No cuts and bulges, 1.6 mm of tread depth across the central three-quarters of the breadth of the tyre and around the entire outer circumference.

7. **Show me how you would check that the horn is working (off road only).**

Check is carried out by using control (turn on ignition if necessary).

8. **Open the bonnet, identify where you would check the engine coolant level and tell me how you would check that the engine has the correct level.**

Identify high- and low-level markings on header tank where fitted or radiator filler cap, and describe how to top up to correct level.

9. **Show me how you would check the parking brake for excessive wear.**

Demonstrate by applying parking brake that when it is fully applied it secures itself, and is not at the end of the working travel.

10. **Show me how you would clean the windscreen using the windscreen washer and wipers.**

Operate control to wash and wipe windscreen (turn ignition on if necessary).

11. **Show me how you would set the demister controls to clear all the windows effectively, this should include both front and rear screens.**

Set all relevant controls including fan, temperature, air direction/source and heated screen to clear windscreen and windows. Engine does not have to be started for this demonstration.

12. **Show me how you would switch on the rear fog lights and explain when you would use it/them (no need to exit vehicle).**

Operate switch (turn on dipped headlights and ignition if necessary). Check warning light is on. Explain use.

13. **Show me how you switch your headlight from dipped to main beam and explain how you would know the main beam is on whilst inside the car.**

Operate switch (with ignition or engine on if necessary), check with main beam warning light.

14. **Show me how you would check that the brake lights are working on this vehicle (I can assist you if you need to switch the ignition on but please do not start the engine).**

   Operate brake pedal, make use of reflections in windows, garage door and so on or ask someone to help.

15. **Tell me how you make sure your head restraint is correctly adjusted so it provides the best protection in the event of a crash.**

   The head restraint should be adjusted so the rigid part of the head restraint is at least as high as the eye or top of the ears, and as close to the back of the head as is comfortable. Some restraints might not be adjustable.

Learning to drive, ride or simply want to brush up on your knowledge?

- All the latest revision questions and answers
- Over 100 high-quality hazard perception clips
- Accessible on any internet-connected device

Visit **www.dvsalearningzone.co.uk** and enter code **SD10** to save 10%.

Revise on the go!

The Official DVSA Theory Test Kit for Car Drivers app

Give yourself the best chance of passing first time with the only Official DVSA Theory Test Kit app.

For everyone!

The Official DVSA Highway Code iPhone app

All the rules of the road at your fingertips.

The Official DVSA Hazard Perception Practice app

The simple and convenient way to prepare for your hazard perception test on the go.

SAVE 10% on official DVSA publications

Get ready to pass your theory and practical tests. Shop now at **www.safedrivingforlife.info/shop** and enter code **SD10** to **SAVE 10%** or call **01603 696979** quoting **SD10.***

 safedrivinglife   @safedrivinglife   safedrivingforlifeinfo   safe.driving.for.life

TSO (The Stationery Office) is proud to be DVSA's official publishing partner. TSO pays for the marketing of all the products we publish. Images are correct at time of going to press but subject to change without notice. The Stationery Office Limited is registered in England No. 3049649 at 1–5 Poland Street, Soho, London, W1F 8PR. *Please note smartphone apps and ebooks are not included in the promotional discount.